Jessie Anand
in association with Walrus Theatre

YELLOWFIN

MAREK HORN

The first performance of *Yellowfin*
was at Southwark Playhouse, London
on 13 October 2021

YELLOWFIN

By Marek Horn

Marianne	Nancy Crane
Roy	Nicholas Day
Calantini	Joshua James
Stephen	Beruce Khan

Director	Ed Madden
Set and Costume Designer	Anisha Fields
Lighting Designer	Rajiv Pattani
Sound Designer	Max Pappenheim
Assistant Director	Charlotte Vickers
Production Manager	Zara Janmohamed
Stage Manager	Cassie Harrison
Producer	Jessie Anand

Additional Casting	Jacob Sparrow

Press	Chloé Nelkin Consulting
Marketing	Cup of Ambition

With thanks to the Arts Patrons Trust, the Bryan Guinness
Charitable Trust, the Golsoncott Foundation, the Royal
Victoria Hall Foundation, the Unity Theatre Trust,
Avye Leventis and Patrick Marber.

Marek Horn

Marek Horn is a playwright based in London. His debut play, *Wild Swimming*, premiered at the 2019 Edinburgh Festival Fringe in a production by FullRogue Theatre, having received a Pleasance Regional Partnership Award, a Ronald Duncan Prize and a Bristol Old Vic Ferment Commission. It later enjoyed a sell-out run at Bristol Old Vic, and will return for a national tour. A radio version was commissioned by BBC Radio 4 for their 2020 schedule. Marek was shortlisted for Out of Joint's Inaugural WiT Award in 2017, and the Barbican's Oxford Samuel Beckett Theatre Trust Award in 2018. He is Playwright on Attachment at Bristol Old Vic.

Nancy Crane

Nancy's stage credits include *Summer and Smoke*, *Chimerica* (Almeida/West End); *Dance Nation*, *Against* (Almeida); *The Sewing Group*, *Now or Later*, *The Sweetest Swing in Baseball* (Royal Court); *Teddy Ferrara* (Donmar Warehouse); *The Children's Hour* (West End); *Design for Living* (Old Vic); *Love the Sinner*, *Angels in America* (National Theatre). Television work includes *Inside Man* (BBC/Netflix); *The Power* (Amazon); *Call the Midwife* (BBC); *Avenue 5* (HBO/Sky Atlantic); *Black Earth Rising* (BBC/Netflix) and *Patrick Melrose* (Showtime/Sky Atlantic). Film includes *The Current War*, *The Danish Girl* and *The Dark Knight*.

Nicholas Day

Nicholas' theatre work includes *Romeo and Juliet*, *Cardenio*, *The Tempest*, *Twelfth Night*, *Dido Queen of Carthage*, *Vice Versa* (RSC); *Wolf Hall* (RSC/West End/Broadway); *The Wild Duck* (Almeida); *Platonov* (Chichester/National Theatre); *The History Boys* (Sheffield Crucible); *The Country Wife* (West End); *Hecuba* (Donmar Warehouse); David Hare trilogy (National Theatre); *Dealer's Choice* (National Theatre/West End/international tour); *Boy Gets Girl* (Royal Court); *An Inspector Calls* (national tour); *The Country Girl* (West End); *The Iceman Cometh* (Almeida/Old Vic). Television includes *The Crown*, *Brexit*, *Poirot*, *The Take*, *Midsomer Murders*, *Foyle's War*, *Doc Martin*, *New Tricks*, *Cambridge Spies*, *Trouble in Mind*, *The Lakes*, *Kavanagh QC*, *Minder*, *Harry's Game*. Film includes *The Wolfman*, *Amazing Grace*, *Les Poupées Russes*, *The Golden Bowl*. Documentary includes *Myths & Monsters*, *Murder Maps*, *Railway Murders*.

Beruce Khan

Beruce's recent stage credits include *Adult Children* (Donmar Warehouse); *Neville's Island* (Queen's, Hornchurch); *Ravens* (Hampstead), and his other credits include *Shadowlands* in Chichester opposite Hugh Bonneville; a number of seasons at the RSC including *A Christmas Carol* and *Twelfth Night*; *Henry V* and *As You Like It* at Regent's Park Open Air Theatre; and major roles in the West End and at the National Theatre. He also played Laertes on the Globe's two-year tour of *Hamlet*, which played in every country in the world. Recent TV work includes *War of the Worlds* (Canal+); *Canoe* (ITV) and *Britannia* (Sky/Amazon Prime).

Joshua James

Joshua's recent theatre credits include: *Wife* (Kiln); *Anna X* (VAULT Festival); *Lady Windermere's Fan* (West End); *Life of Galileo* (Young Vic); *Platonov/The Seagull, Here We Go, Light Shining in Buckinghamshire, Treasure Island* (National Theatre); *Fathers and Sons* (Donmar Warehouse); *The Ritual Slaughter of Gorge Mastromas, No Quarter, Love and Information* (Royal Court) and *Wolf Hall/Bring Up The Bodies* (RSC). TV credits include: *Why Didn't They Ask Evans?* (Britbox); *The Ipcress File* (ITV); *I Hate Suzie* (Sky/Bad Wolf); *Life* (BBC/Drama Republic); *Industry* (HBO/Bad Wolf); *Black Mirror* (Netflix) and *Raised by Wolves* (TNT/Scott Free). Film credits include: *Cyrano* (Working Title/MGM); *Darkest Hour* (Working Title) and *Criminal* (Millennium Films).

Ed Madden

For Walrus, Ed has directed *A Table Tennis Play* and *Lemons Lemons Lemons Lemons Lemons*. Other directing credits include: *A Number* (The Other Room); *The World's Wife* (Welsh National Opera and touring). Work as assistant director includes: *Leopoldstadt* (West End); *Tartuffe* (National Theatre); *The Winter's Tale* (Shakespeare's Globe); *The Children* (Royal Court); *The Rivals* (Bristol Old Vic/Glasgow Citizens/Liverpool Everyman & Playhouse); *The Iphigenia Quartet* (Gate).

Anisha Fields

Anisha is a graduate of Bristol Old Vic Theatre School. She was a recipient of the Leverhulme Arts Scholarship, resident at the RSC 2018-19. She was also named as one of the Guardian's 12 theatre stars to watch for 2020. Anisha is an Associate Artist at Theatre Iolo. Recent and upcoming design credits include *Acis and Galatea* (Early Opera Company); *The Lower Depths* (RCSSD); *Squirrel* (the egg, Theatre Royal Bath); *Who's Afraid of Virginia Woolf* (Tobacco Factory/Salisbury Playhouse); *First Encounters: Merchant of Venice* (RSC); *Owl at Home* (Theatre Iolo); *I Wish I Was A Mountain* (the egg/Travelling Light) and *Beautiful Thing*, *A View from the Bridge* and *Macbeth* (Tobacco Factory). As associate: *Camp Siegfried* (Old Vic).

Rajiv Pattani
Rajiv graduated from LAMDA in 2014 with qualifications in Stage Management and Technical Theatre. Recent design work includes: *Santi & Nas*, *Omelette*, *Heroine*, *Tiger Mum*, *10* (VAULT Festival); *Hunger* (Arcola); *Dirty Crusty* (Yard); *Dismantle This Room* (Royal Court); *Wolfie* (Theatre503); *Babylon Beyond Borders*, *Leave Taking*, *Dismantle This Room* (Bush); *Bullet Hole* (Park); *Roman Candle* (Theatre503/Manchester 53Two/Edinburgh Fringe).

Max Pappenheim
Max is a sound designer and composer based in London. He is an Associate Artist of The Faction. Theatre includes *Cruise*, *The Night of the Iguana* (West End); *Assembly*, *The Way of the World* (Donmar Warehouse); *The Children* (Royal Court/Broadway); *Macbeth* (Chichester Festival Theatre); *Crooked Dances* (RSC); *Dry Powder*, *Labyrinth* (Hampstead); *Ophelias Zimmer* (Schaubühne, Berlin/Royal Court); *One Night in Miami* (Nottingham Playhouse); *Hogarth's Progress* (Rose, Kingston); *The Ridiculous Darkness* (Gate); *Amsterdam*, Blue/Heart (Orange Tree); *The Tempest*, *Beckett Triple Bill* (Jermyn Street Theatre); *The Gaul* (Hull Truck); *Jane Wenham* (Out of Joint); *Waiting for Godot* (Sheffield Crucible); *My Eyes Went Dark* (Traverse/59E59, New York); *The Cardinal*, *Kiki's Delivery Service* (Southwark Playhouse); *Looking Good Dead*, *The Habit of Art* (national tours). Opera includes *Miranda* (Opéra Comique, Paris); *Scraww* (Trebah Gardens); *Vixen* (Vaults/international tour); *Carmen: Remastered* (Royal Opera House/Barbican). Film includes *The Haunting of Alice Bowles*; *Barnes' People* (Original Online). Dance includes *While You Are Here* (DanceEast/The Place).

Charlotte Vickers

Charlotte is a director and fundraiser with a particular interest in how art can be used to challenge preconceptions and create new worlds, and in making the arts themselves a safer and fairer place. Recent directing work includes *Andromeda* (Camden People's Theatre/Nottingham Playhouse) and *Edward II* (Oxford Playhouse). She has workshopped and developed plays at Theatre503, the Young Vic and the White Bear Theatre, and trained on the Catalyst programme at the North Wall Arts Centre. She works as a fundraiser for national charity Arts Emergency, and is currently studying for an MA in Gender, Media and Culture at Goldsmiths University.

Jessie Anand Productions

Jessie Anand Productions makes theatre and opera that is fresh and playful. Since it was founded in 2018, it has produced three new plays, *MAGDALENE* by Mary Galloway (Arcola Theatre); *Orlando* by Lucy Roslyn (VAULT Festival/Edinburgh Fringe) and the site-specific piece *Blue Thunder*, which played a sold-out run at VAULT Festival in 2019 and has since been adapted for BBC Radio 4.

The company's opera work includes *Cabildo* (Wilton's Music Hall/Arcola Theatre) and a digital production of *The Telephone* in partnership with Guildhall School of Music and Drama.

Projects currently in development include Lucy Roslyn's new play *Pennyroyal* and Maz O'Connor's musical *The Wife of Michael Cleary*.

Jessie Anand Productions is supported by Stage One.

Walrus

Walrus is a theatre company dedicated to new writing, led by director and dramaturg Ed Madden. The company's award-winning debut production, Sam Steiner's play *Lemons Lemons Lemons Lemons Lemons*, premiered in 2015, before selling out three consecutive Edinburgh Fringe runs and embarking on a major UK tour. *A Table Tennis Play*, also by Sam Steiner, played to critical acclaim at the Edinburgh Fringe in 2019.

YELLOWFIN

Marek Horn

For my friend, Ed Madden

…let the record show.

2

Author's Note

I wrote this play several years ago now, back when I was clueless and terrified. With that in mind, I'd like to thank all the people who supported me when I was most in need of their help. In particular, I owe a debt of gratitude to Clive Judd, Stewart Pringle, Gus Miller and James Peries for championing my work and for supporting my early development. I am also grateful to Clive and Julia Lampard and to Nikki and Dez Franklin for giving me a home from home, in London and Bristol, whenever I was in need.

I've learnt a little since then; mainly that the troughs are as deep as the peaks are high. With that in mind, thank you to Dan, Ellie, Euan, Beth, Mim, Marietta, Stuart and Sam for keeping me sane; to my family for keeping their faith; to Maxine for her certainty that things would come good and to Sue, for reminding me that there is more to life than fucking plays. Most importantly, however, I would like to say thank you to Becky, for making every day better, whatever the weather.

Finally, I would like to express my enduring gratitude to Nancy, Nick, Josh, Beruce, Cassie and Charlotte for making the rehearsal of this play so blissfully fulfilling; to Jessi Stewart for being a spectacular agent; to Jessie Anand for working so hard to get this play on, and to Ed Madden for directing *Yellowfin* to the best of his abilities. Ed has been there since the beginning and has helped me both to savour the triumphs and laugh off the defeats. I am impossibly grateful to the little fella; to have worked with him on this, so closely and for so long, has been a joy and a privilege.

Marek Horn

Director's Note

Marek sent me a three-sentence synopsis of *Yellowfin* on 4
October 2015 and completed a first draft nine days later –
exactly six years before it will have its premiere. He couldn't
have known that a year on, *post-truth* would be named Oxford
Word of the Year, nor that three years after that the phrase
climate emergency would claim the same accolade. He was
too early – a week and a half – to take inspiration from Hillary
Clinton's eleven-hour testimony before the House Select
Committee on Benghazi, let alone to have drawn on the
Senate hearings of James Comey, Mark Zuckerberg and Brett
Kavanaugh which would go on to grip the world; and though, as
a history buff, he could grasp the potential of national myths to
influence electorates, he was nevertheless writing at a time when
the eventual outcomes of the 2016 EU Referendum and US
Presidential Election were at surpassingly long odds.

How then is his play somehow about all of these things? Or, I
should say, about all of what these things were about? The best
answer came from Nancy Crane, who plays Marianne in our
production, when she remarked: 'It's about words, really about
words.' So simple, and so true. In a way which gets to the crux
of many of the phenomena of the past six years, *Yellowfin* is
interested in words as the building blocks of how we describe,
process and interpret the world around us – its wit is to turn up
the heat on that concern by way of a central conceit so sense-
shatteringly absurd as to defy articulation or explanation.

All of the play's characters wield language as a tool not only to
attempt to describe reality, but to create it; to reframe the past,
lay claim to the present, and build the future. What their writer
understands is that this tool is just as potent – maybe even more
so – when language is comic as when it is sincere, evasive,
domineering, wistful. I am writing this early in rehearsals, after

a day which has been characterised in the main by all kinds of laughter. It is simply a pleasure to work with actors so brilliant on writing so rich.

Much of the first draft of *Yellowfin* is still recognisable in this published text – it hasn't been periodically revised for topicality – but in the too-long span of time that Marek has been waiting for it to find its rightful home on stage, he has honed it to a fine edge, a sashimi knife of a play. It is ready to meet its audiences. I hope that it will continue to meet them for a long time. Perhaps, however frighteningly, it will only grow in relevance, and my instinct that it might be especially apposite to the moment of its first production will come to seem quaint and naïve. We will have to see. Keep an eye on your fish.

Ed Madden, September 2021

The power of myth is in making meaning
from the wreckage of meaning.

John Gray – *The Silence of Animals*

We possess nothing certainly, except the past.

Evelyn Waugh – *Brideshead Revisited*

Characters

CALANTINI, *a man called Calantini. He is about thirty-five*

MARIANNE, *The Senator. A member of the United States Senate, should be scary and authoritative, and about sixty*

ROY, *The Other Senator. Another member of the Senate, older, in his eighties, a drowsy and avuncular presence*

STEPHEN, *The Other Other Senator. Another, younger politician, about forty and has ambitions beyond the Senate. He is reasonably handsome and greying*

The Space

The setting is a room on Capitol Hill – not grand, but with allusions towards grandeur, with flags and Seals of Office and suchlike adorning the space. Generic water decanters and glasses should be available for all, and probably also coffee and biscuits (old stale coffee and old stale biscuits) that nobody but Roy should ever touch. There should be two exits: A set of large grand double doors, and a fire exit.

In my head the stage is set up for traverse, with a long table at one end at which Calantini sits. At the other end should be a raised bench or desk at which the three senators sit – Marianne in the middle, with Roy to her left and Stephen to her right – like judges, bearing down.

The most crucial element is the microphones. Each character should have a table-top microphone placed in front of them. The purpose of these in the world of the play is primarily to record, but for our purposes they should also amplify and be very sensitive to changes in intensity and volume. Mediated sound is the play's key aesthetic element. It is a stationary play, in the main, and so elements like sound texture become incredibly important. I will indicate in the script moments where I feel a particular change is needed, people talking or shouting directly into a mic or pulling their head away, perhaps moving away completely. These should not be thought prescriptive, however. I would encourage the cast and director to follow my lead and play with what textures and intensities can be discovered and conveyed.

A Note on the Delivery

Key words would be 'dry', 'formal', 'detached' and 'ironic'. The language at times is very heightened and arch and so any urge towards melodrama should be resisted. Speak quickly, or else portentousness might seep through.

A '*Pause*' or a '*Beat*' denotes a break in the rhythm of discourse. A Beat is a short and rhythmic Pause. A '*Silence*', however short, suggests the absence of the desire to speak.

This text went to press before the end of rehearsals and so may differ slightly from the play as performed.

ACT ONE

Scene One

MARIANNE. So… describe to me how the pure grade
    …*Fish substance*…
    The *wild* fish substance
    Came to be contaminated?

*CALANTINI is sat back in his chair. He sighs, and then
moves close to the mic, eyeballing the Senator before
speaking.*

CALANTINI. I'm sorry but…
    Perhaps you could just say tuna fish?

Beat.

Because… we know what you mean

MARIANNE. I'm aware of that, Mr Calantini

CALANTINI. Everyone knows what you mean

MARIANNE. Thank you, Mr Calantini
    I am aware

CALANTINI. Well then…

MARIANNE. Well then?
    Well then, what?

CALANTINI. Well then…
    Nothing

Pause.

MARIANNE. It's quite a big deal
    This
    Y'know?
    Getting hauled up in front of a Senate Committee like this
    You know that, don't you?

It's a big deal

A beat and then close in to mic.

CALANTINI. I know that

MARIANNE. That doesn't happen to everyone
That doesn't happen every day

Again, another beat and then very close in to mic.

CALANTINI. I know

MARIANNE. And
If we find the testimonial you provide us with today to be in any way unsatisfactory…

STEPHEN. Or a little too satisfactory perhaps

MARIANNE. Yes indeed
Yes quite, thank you, Stephen
If we find either one or the other
If, either, we discover something new
Or
And this is crucial
Or if we think you're *hiding* something
A full Congressional Hearing *will* follow

Again, CALANTINI *sighs and then moves close in to the mic in an insolent way.*

CALANTINI. I understand that

MARIANNE. And that could lead to public prosecution

Close into the mic.

CALANTINI. Yes

STEPHEN. And you don't want to go back to prison, do you, Mr Calantini?

A pause, a sigh and then close in to the mic.

CALANTINI. No

MARIANNE. Then please confirm that you appreciate the severity of our undertaking here today

CALANTINI. And there…
There's that language again

Into mic, an order.

MARIANNE. Confirm it!

Into mic, an order.

STEPHEN. Confirm it, please

CALANTINI. I confirm it!
Sorry!
Jesus…

Into mic.

Let the record show that
I confirm it…

Into mic.

STEPHEN *and* ROY. Let the record show

Relaxing, leaning back in chair.

MARIANNE. Let the record show

Beat.

Thank you, Mr Calantini
Now please
Continue to demonstrate respect and conscientiousness for
the duration of our undertaking here today

CALANTINI. I will

MARIANNE. Thank you

CALANTINI. It wasn't contaminated

Beat.

MARIANNE. I'm sorry?

Right into the mic.

CALANTINI. It wasn't contaminated
    The fish that my brother sold to the Russians
    You asked me how it became contaminated, but it wasn't
    They said it was
    The Russians said it was
    But it wasn't

    Beat.

MARIANNE. Alright then, explain to me how, Mr Calantini,
    Explain to me how *these accusations*
    These accusations that were levelled against you and your
    late brother by *these Russians*
    Explain to me how they were, in fact, erroneous
    In what way were they erroneous?

CALANTINI. I'm sorry...
    I'm sorry but
    Madame Senator, I appreciate *your* position here today?
    And
    I appreciate *my* position here today?
    But this language is unnecessary
    This language is causing me
    Agitation
    I mean, this isn't meant to be snooty, but who exactly do you
    think you're talking to?

MARIANNE. Excuse me?

CALANTINI. I'm not The King of fuckin' England y'know?
    I don't need this special *'highfalutin'* language to be directed
    at me
    It makes me agitated

MARIANNE. We have certain procedures here, Mr Calantini
    A procedural way of processing the information we're given
    The language we use is not intended to alienate you...

ROY. He's dead

    Beat.

STEPHEN. Sorry Roy, what was that?

Softly, into the mic.

ROY. The King of England
    He's dead

MARIANNE. Roy, please…

STEPHEN. Thank you for that, Roy

CALANTINI. No
    No, your man here is right
    He is dead
    They're all dead
    They're all gone
    Who are you trying to impress?!

MARIANNE. I won't continue to have this argument with you,
    Mr Calantini
    It is not an effective use of our time

CALANTINI. But…

MARIANNE. And we *will* use this time effectively, Mr
    Calantini
    You can be sure of that
    Let the record show *that*, at the very least

Into the mic, murmuring assent.

ROY. Let the record show

STEPHEN. You say their claim was erroneous…
    How so, Mr Calantini?

CALANTINI. Wrong?
    You mean wrong?
    You mean 'mistaken' right?

MARIANNE. Yes.
    Mr Calantini, what led them to make that mistake?

CALANTINI. I don't know what led them to make that mistake
    I can't speak to that

STEPHEN. You can't speak to that?

CALANTINI. I can't speak to that, no sir

STEPHEN. You can't speak to that?
    Or you won't speak to that?

CALANTINI. It's not my area
    I only know that he,
    My brother,
    He didn't do what they said he did

STEPHEN. Right…
    Well, that doesn't help us

CALANTINI. It's the truth

MARIANNE. Be more expansive
    Please
    Be more expansive with your truth

CALANTINI. More's to the point,
    More's to the actual fucking point,
    Not only did he not do it –
    Because he didn't do it

MARIANNE. Noted, for the sake of the record

    Right into the mic.

STEPHEN. Let the record show

CALANTINI. Not only did he not do it, but it would have been
    unthinkable for him *to have had* done it
    There would be no way that he could have done what they
    said he did, and for him to think he'd get away with it
    It would have been suicide
    He wouldn't have been so stupid

MARIANNE. Right, so you're saying he didn't cut

    Searching her notes and then reading.

    'Pure Skipjack steak'…

CALANTINI. No
    No you're wrong
    Your facts are wrong

MARIANNE. I'm sorry?

He sighs.

CALANTINI. Was this little tribunal assembled somewhat
    hastily, perchance, Madam Senator?

Pause, she glowers at him.

MARIANNE. What's the mistake, Mr Calantini?
    Please enlighten us
    As to our error

CALANTINI. It wasn't Skipjack
    No one would go that nuts for Skipjack...
    These people...
    They wouldn't be *eating* Skipjack

MARIANNE. No?

CALANTINI. No

MARIANNE. Well what was it, then?

ROY. Bluefin?

CALANTINI. What?

Suddenly uncertain.

ROY. Was it maybe...
    Bluefin?

Beat.

CALANTINI. No
    Don't be so stupid

ROY. Excuse me, young man?

MARIANNE. Yes, Roy, don't be stupid

ROY. What?
    What did I say?

STEPHEN. If it was Bluefin, Roy, we'd know about it…
We'd all know about it

ROY. Yeah but…

MARIANNE. Enough!
Please!

A pause as she eyeballs ROY. *She then gestures to*
CALANTINI *to continue.*

Please

CALANTINI. It was Yellowfin
Sashimi Grade
I think

MARIANNE. Thank you
Not *Bluefin,* Roy
…Preposterous suggestion

ROY. Alright
Whatever

STEPHEN. That's good though right, Sashimi Grade?
That's

Very much into the mic for this one.

Good Fish

CALANTINI. Yes. It's the best kind of Yellowfin,
Second-best kind of tuna,
Second only to Bluefin

STEPHEN. And it was canned?

Beat and then into the mic.

CALANTINI.…Yeah

MARIANNE. Yes

Beat. STEPHEN *thinks.*

STEPHEN. Does that not strike you as a little… odd?

MARIANNE. In what way?

CALANTINI. Yeah, in what way?

MARIANNE. Ah, thank you, Mr Calantini, we'll ask the questions

Beat.

Stephen?

STEPHEN. Forgive me, but...
Leaving aside the question of the disputed contamination for a second
Just, holding that in your mind over to one side, for a second
I'm interested...

MARIANNE. This better be good, Stephen

STEPHEN. I'm interested in how something *that good* gets into a can

Beat.

Skipjack goes in the can, sure
Bigeye and Blackfin goes in the can, sure thing
But Sashimi Grade Yellowfin?
Surely that would've been sold for fresh, would it not?

Beat.

CALANTINI. Generally speaking... I guess it would
Yeah

STEPHEN. Right...

CALANTINI. I'm not a historian. I can't speak to the particulars but yeah
I guess it would

STEPHEN. So what's it doing in the can?

CALANTINI *shrugs.*

CALANTINI. I don't know what it's doing in the can
We got lucky, I guess
What else can I say?

STEPHEN. Sorry, you got
You got... lucky?

CALANTINI. My brother was a lucky guy…
    Until he wasn't

    Pause, STEPHEN *changes tack.*

STEPHEN. Okay, fine
    So you got lucky

CALANTINI. Like I said, he was a lucky guy

STEPHEN. Sure
    But even so
    How do you know?

    Beat.

CALANTINI. How do I know what?

STEPHEN. How do you know how lucky you got?

    Beat.

    Let's just imagine, for one moment, that yes, alright, all those
    years ago
    At some point before the fish went away
    They put Sashimi Grade Yellowfin in a can
    Even so…
    It's… *what… thirty… thirty-five years old*, at least?

CALANTINI. Oh sure, at least

STEPHEN. And it's cooked, right?

    Right into the mic, deliberate.

CALANTINI. Right

MARIANNE. What's your point, Stephen?

STEPHEN. Well, how do you know what it is?
    How do you know that something is 'Sashimi Grade'?
    Whatever that means
    When it's cooked
    And
    Thirty-five years old
    And

Let's not forget
Inside an airtight tin can?

Beat, and then into the mic.

CALANTINI. You just know

STEPHEN. You just...?

Into the mic.

CALANTINI. You just know, sir

STEPHEN. Right

Beat.

Would you care to elaborate on that or...?

CALANTINI. There are ways of finding out

STEPHEN. Right?

Pregnant pause, and then into the mic.

CALANTINI. ...Yeah

Pause. Into the mic.

STEPHEN. You're under oath, Mr Calantini

CALANTINI. ...Yeah

STEPHEN. So please speak to that...
Please expand on that...
For the record

CALANTINI. It's a secret

STEPHEN. That's not our concern

CALANTINI. It's a family secret

STEPHEN. Excuse me?

Beat. Into the mic.

CALANTINI. It's a family
Secret

STEPHEN. A family secret?

CALANTINI. Yeah

STEPHEN. A *family* secret?

> *Into the mic.*

CALANTINI.…Yeah!

STEPHEN. Right
> And what family would that be, Mr Calantini?
> What family are you trying to protect?

> *Pause.*

ROY. Jesus Christ, Stephen
> Go easy, will yah?

CALANTINI. You're a piece of shit, y'know that?

STEPHEN. Yeah? Well, let the record show that, too, I guess

> ROY *speaks to himself.*

ROY. Let the record show
> Jesus fuck

STEPHEN. Nevertheless, I am waiting, Mr Calantini
> How do you know
> That the fish in the can
> Is Sashimi Grade?

> CALANTINI *sighs. Pause.*

CALANTINI. Firstly you weigh it,
> To ascertain fluid retention and fat content,
> And then you x-ray it, the can I mean,
> And then you magnify the x-rays
> And you look at them…
> Closely
> And
> Repeatedly
> And
> That way you judge the quality of the *flakeage*

Into the mic.

STEPHEN. I'm sorry the what?
What was that?

Beat, then into the mic.

CALANTINI. The *'Flakeage'*

STEPHEN. The Flakeage?

CALANTINI. Yes

Slowly, into the mic.

Flakeage

STEPHEN. Expand on that, please
For the record

CALANTINI. Simply put, a better quality tuna fish will have a
more fibrous muscle structure

Beat.

Or something
I guess
…I dunno

STEPHEN. Right

CALANTINI. That was my brother's area of expertise, not mine
I was just the front man
Look is all this really necessary?

STEPHEN. This tribunal has reason to believe that it might be
pertinent, yes

CALANTINI. Right

Softly, deep in thought.

MARIANNE. No…

Beat, into the mic.

CALANTINI. Sorry, what was that?
Please?

STEPHEN. Marianne?

MARIANNE. No actually it doesn't
    No it isn't

The following is all away from microphone, perhaps
MARIANNE *even puts her hand over the microphone,*
striking a confidential, conspiratorial tone.

What are you getting at, Stephen?

STEPHEN. I'm not getting at anything...

MARIANNE. I think that you are

CALANTINI. Excuse me...

STEPHEN. Well I'm not
    I'm just trying to patch up the holes, that's all
    What's the issue?

MARIANNE. You're overstepping the mark

STEPHEN. What?

CALANTINI. Excuse me, sorry

MARIANNE. Due process will be observed, Stephen

STEPHEN. Well what's that supposed to mean?

MARIANNE. Due process will be observed
    Give it time

CALANTINI. Sorry...
    Is there an issue?

Into the mic.

MARIANNE. Your patience is appreciated, Mr Calantini

Away from the mic.

You know what I mean, Stephen

CALANTINI. Am I missing something here?
    Is there an issue that I should be made aware of?

MARIANNE *gives* STEPHEN *a severe look. Pause. They return to talking at the microphone, compensating by coming in close.*

MARIANNE. None

MARIANNE *and* STEPHEN *eyeball each other, until* STEPHEN *yields.*

STEPHEN. None whatsoever

Beat, and then very close to microphone.

I have completed my line of enquiry

MARIANNE. Thank you, senator

To dissipate the tension, papers are shuffled and water is drunk.

Now, perhaps, we might return to the issue of the disputed contamination…

ROY. How do you know…
…That it was all one fish?

Beat.

MARIANNE. *Roy…*

CALANTINI. I'm sorry, sir
…What?

ROY. If it's a can of tuna
How do you know that all the tuna in there is the same tuna?
This special 'Sashimi Grade', 'Yellowfin' tuna?

Beat.

CALANTINI. How do you mean, sir…?

MARIANNE. *Roy, for goodness' sake*

ROY. Well… it's chunks, right?
Canned fish comes in chunks, does it not?
At the end of the day, these are just a load of
Old chunks
Of fish
Right?

CALANTINI. This was a steak, sir

ROY. Sorry?

Loudly and clearly into the mic, patronising.

CALANTINI. This wasn't chunks, sir?
This was a steak?

Beat, he sighs.

There are two kinds of canned fish
If you don't care what you're giving people
And
You want to maximise the use of space in the can
You chunk it
If you want to go slightly higher up the food chain, if you're interested in quality, then you would… This is historically speaking,
This is me speaking historically

ROY. Noted, thank you
For the sake of the record

CALANTINI. Historically speaking…
You would
One would
Have wanted to retain the integrity of the fish's natural structure… in some way

ROY. Well alright, but…
Sorry, I'm a little confused…

Close in to mic.

CALANTINI. Not at all
You go right ahead

MARIANNE. No, please, can we…?

STEPHEN. I think… just to speed the plough here for a second
I think what my colleague is alluding to is that…
These fish would have been canned at a time when fresh stocks were still thought readily available, am I right?

CALANTINI. That is correct

STEPHEN. Right, well, I think what's foxing the senior senator from Illinois, here, is why someone would spend any extra money on something just because it was... *intact*?
Especially when you could have just gone and bought a fresh tuna steak from the store
Is that about the nub of it, Roy?

ROY. Yes, thank you, Stephen
That is my question exactly

CALANTINI. I can't answer to that

STEPHEN. You can't answer to that?

CALANTINI. I can't answer to that because I'm not an historian, okay?
Historically that is what they would have done, but I'm not an historian so I can't answer to that
I don't know why they did it, I just know that they did
Sometimes they chunked it and sometimes they left it as a steak

Beat.

I think it was an English thing or something...
Some hangover from the war, I guess
From the big one that they had
The second one, with the Germans
Back then fresh fish wasn't available I guess... because of all the Germans
And their aggression
...And the existential threat that they posed
But...
I don't know
That's all I can say on the matter

MARIANNE. That's all you can say?

CALANTINI. That's all I can say
I can't speak to the matter any more than that
It's not my area

MARIANNE. Right, well perhaps we can get someone to look
into that at a more *convenient* time
We have it on the record so, I guess, at a more convenient
moment…

From deep thought, interrupting.

ROY. It was salmon, I think

Pause, MARIANNE *and* STEPHEN *share a wary, weary
look.*

STEPHEN. Sorry, Roy?

ROY. The English, in the nineteen-fifties
If I remember correctly
Would go cock-a-hoop over canned Salmon
My father, he grew up over there, you see
He was a boy there
And
Now that you mention it, I remember him telling me…
You'd open up a can of salmon on someone's birthday or
their wedding or something
Because it was a special occasion
And
Well
I guess, *because* it was a special occasion, you'd want it to
look like real fish,
Like fresh fish,
You'd want it to look like it had just come out of the sea
You'd want it to look like
It had just come out
…*Of a fish*
Right?

Beat

CALANTINI. Yes sir, I would say that is exactly right

ROY. Right
Alright
And so, with that in mind, a full steak would've been
preferable to fish chunks, I guess
Because a steak… you can… *flourish* it, can't you?

CALANTINI. Sure

ROY. Garnish it
   Sprinkle it
   With
   Parsley
   And
   Black pepper
   And
   Vinegar

   Beat, and then into the mic.

CALANTINI. *Sure*

MARIANNE. Right...

ROY. And so
   Although chunking is easier
   And
   Cheaper
   And
   More economic,
   I guess a canned steak gained a sense of status which stuck
   Even though the war was over
   And the existential threat diminished
   And the great English empire soon long dead and gone
   That sense of status stuck
   Whether you were English or not
   Whether it was salmon or not
   It persisted
   That... special status persisted
   Just like it still does today
   Just like it did with those *Russians* of yours

   Pause.

MARIANNE. Alright, well as *enlightening* as all this is...

ROY. I miss the English

MARIANNE. Right...

ROY. They were a *strange* people, you know?

MARIANNE. Okay

ROY. My father's family were English,

MARIANNE. Thank you, Roy

ROY. Scottish actually,
     But they lived in England, at the time

CALANTINI. I'm sorry to hear that

MARIANNE. Mr Calantini, please

CALANTINI. *Were they all drowned?*

ROY. They were
     They were all drowned

CALANTINI. I'm sorry

ROY. Thank you,
     Thank you, young man

     Pause.

MARIANNE. Right…
     Can we?

     Into the mic.

STEPHEN. Let the record show that I too am sorry.

MARIANNE. Stephen…

     Into the mic.

CALANTINI. Let the record show that

     Into the mic.

STEPHEN. Yes, let the record show

     Into the mic.

CALANTINI, ROY *and* STEPHEN. Let the record show

MARIANNE. Yes!
    Fine!
    We're all sorry
    Sorry, sorry, sorry!
    Let the record show!
    Jesus Christ!

    Beat.

    Now!
    Please!
    Can we get on?
    Please?

    Beat.

ROY. Sorry, Marianne

STEPHEN. Sorry, Marianne

    Into the mic.

CALANTINI. Sorry… *Marianne*

    Pause. She sighs.

MARIANNE. So we know it was one fish…?
    You're certain it was a steak and not chunks that your brother
    was dealing with, Mr Calantini?

CALANTINI. Yes
    Let the record show that

MARIANNE. How can you be sure?

CALANTINI. How can I be *sure*?

MARIANNE. You claim that the can was opened in your
    absence
    How can you be so sure of its contents?

    Beat.

CALANTINI. These guys…
    These guys weren't English
    Okay?
    They weren't of a placid temperament like the English
    They were Russian

MARIANNE. Right

CALANTINI. There are plenty of Russians still hanging around
Too many if you ask me
Too many with unwholesome occupations
…If you ask me

MARIANNE. Yes
Let's not *careen off* onto another tangent, Mr Calantini
Stick to the point please

CALANTINI. Sorry
It's just that people ask me
Under the circumstances, I guess

MARIANNE. *Yes*

CALANTINI. Under the circumstances, I get asked a lot about
Russians

MARIANNE. Yes, and you have our sympathies

Into the mic.

ROY. Let the record show this

MARIANNE. Yes let the record show this,
But please
We must continue
You have our sympathies and now we must continue
Please, go on

Pause. Maybe he pours some water.

CALANTINI. These guys…
These Russian guys
It would have been all about the flakeage with them

STEPHEN. Right and what is *flakeage*?
What does that mean?
Speak to that, please

CALANTINI. Synthetic fish,
Squib-fish as we would call it,
The cloned fish that you and I eat on a daily basis,

We've never been quite able to get the muscle structure right,
The texture is…
Always a little spongy,
A little… *stodgy*,
When compared to the real thing

MARIANNE. The real thing?

CALANTINI. Yes…
Real fish…
Wild fish
The fish that we had before the fish went
It… *flakes*
It's hard to describe how it flakes, but it flakes in a… *magical
way*
Unless you've actually *had* some it's hard to describe what it
means really
For fish
…*To flake*

ROY. I remember fish
Real fish

MARIANNE. As do I… vaguely

CALANTINI. Then you know what I'm talking about?

She shrugs.

MARIANNE.… Vaguely

STEPHEN. Well, for my benefit then
Please

ROY. You don't remember real fish, Stephen?

STEPHEN. I was five, Roy
When they went I was only five

ROY. Oh… right
Y'know, you look older

STEPHEN. Thank you, Roy, I appreciate that
Please, Mr Calantini
For me
For the record

Into the mic.

Speak to flakeage

Pause. He speaks into the mic.

CALANTINI. It's a pulling apart, I guess
  It's a pulling apart... *of strands*
  Fish... y'see
  Real fish, it
  ... *Fragments*
  It... *crumbles*
  It breaks on the tongue like a wave on the shore
  It feels like
  Work
  It feels like
  Nature
  And
  Power
  And
  It feels like a thing... that has lived

Beat.

  I mean, don't get me wrong, our fish live
  The squibs are alive,
  But it's a half-life,
  It can't compare to
  An
  Animal,
  A
  Beast,
  That has
  Ripped
  Through currents
  And
  Torn
  Through storms
  And through salt and pain and cold and space...
  And all that... *toil*
  And

Force
And
Instinct…
It *bleeds* in, I guess, in a sort of
Chemical way

Beat.

On a molecular level
It is captured
In every fleck
It is captured
In every strand
It is captured

Beat.

For most of our clients it's this *texture* that they crave
More than any flavour
Because
Well…
There really is nothing like it

Beat.

And for a dealer
It's my joy, y'know?
That moment when they place it on their tongue is my
pleasure and my pride because
These are nasty people,
They're
Forgive my language

Into the mic.

Unsavoury cunts
As you can imagine…
But seeing their eyes for the first time
When they first try it
It doesn't matter who they are
Their faces light up like a child in the sun
They look free
Like a bird taking flight

It's desire
It's
The transmutation of power
It's
The transmutation of…
Fish
Energy

Beat.

It's an apotheosis and a primal recognition, because a living
thing is on your tongue and wham!

He quickly and loudly slams his hand down on the table.

MARIANNE. *Jesus!*

CALANTINI. It's like sex, really
    It's like a form of sex
    And that's it…
    They're hooked,

Beat.

ROY. Pardon the pun

MARIANNE. Roy!

CALANTINI. The joy on their faces,
    The primal, raw joy at eating something… *real…*
    There really is nothing like it

Beat.

There really was nothing like it
There really *was* nothing like it
I don't deal any more, as you know

ROY. Let the record show

CALANTINI. As you know
    I've gone straight

Close into the mic.

ROY *and* STEPHEN. Let the record show

MARIANNE. Yes well so you say…
    But that's what we're here to ascertain
    Isn't it, Mr Calantini?

Beat.

…Isn't it?

Pause. Into the mic.

CALANTINI.…Apparently so

Beat.

MARIANNE. We will take a recess there

Music. Lights change. Time passes. Lights up.

Scene Two

MARIANNE. So this was a steak then was it?

CALANTINI. Yes, it was a steak

MARIANNE. And good quality
    Yellowfin
    Sashimi Grade

CALANTINI. Yes, preserved in oil not brine,
    And it was intact which was, like I said, part of the appeal
    Which is why the accusation is so completely fuckin'
    ludicrous
    For them to have suggested…
    For them to have *accused* my brother of contaminating it
    Of '*cutting*' it with… what did they say it was…?

Reading from his notes.

STEPHEN.…Pollock

CALANTINI. Yeah Pollock, exactly
    The notion is absurd

STEPHEN. How so?

CALANTINI. Simply put, because there's no 'cutting' to be done
What are you gonna do, hide the Pollock underneath?
It's insane

STEPHEN. But you weren't there?

CALANTINI. I was at the factory
Let the record show that

MARIANNE. Let the record show

STEPHEN. So he could have chunked it, flaked it, whatever,
And then cut it with the Pollock afterwards?

CALANTINI. He wouldn't have done that

STEPHEN. Why not?

CALANTINI. Because he's not a fuckin' moron!
Because he knows what they're after!
He knows what they're paying for!
He knows that *they know* what they're paying for
And he knows that they aren't going to appreciate him
tampering with their fucking meal!

Beat.

Most of them...
When it comes to a can like that,
They want the *complete experience* and he *knew* that
They want to *open it*, themselves
They want to drain the oil over a sink like they're bleeding a
stuck pig
They want to fucking... *hunt* it
They want to feel like they've caught it
Like they *own* it in some primal, spiritual kind of way...
And then
Then
When they've got it in front of them
They want to *flake it* themselves
They want to *rip it* apart

Unlock that energy
That Fish Energy
That history
That wildness
The wild-fish history that is trapped in every strand

Beat.

With all due respect, senator, you have never eaten a fish
You have never *seen* a fish
We had been doing this a long time by this point
He knew what we could get away with

MARIANNE. Which was?

CALANTINI. Nothing
With Russians?
Nothing

STEPHEN. And you're *certain* that he couldn't, in a state of
desperation, have *misguidedly hoped* that they would assume
that he was
Albeit misguidedly
Simply… using his initiative?

CALANTINI. Sir,
You don't fork out two hundred and fifty grand for some
joker to use his initiative
Okay?
Good cooking takes initiative
That takes flair
And
Inventiveness
And
Creativity
Great cooking,
On the other hand,
Great Cooking
Serving Great Food
Is about looking at the absolutely top-flight, weapons-grade
ingredient that you've got in front of you…
Looking at it

Acknowledging its Greatness
And knowing when to stay the fuck out of its way

Beat.

And even if he had wanted to shaft them,
Even if he had been trying to make a quick buck,
He'd have cut the Yellowfin with another tuna,
A Bonito
Or
A Tongol
Or
Considering we were marketing it as Sashimi Grade,
A Bigeye
Big Sushi, big Sashimi fish the Bigeye

MARIANNE. Right

CALANTINI. It's got a higher fat content because they swim
    deeper
    In the colder water, you know?

MARIANNE. Right…

CALANTINI. You could easily pass that off as being
    In some way characteristic of
    In some way indicative of
    A top-flight Yellowfin

Beat.

It would be risky
Because these guys know their shit
And because they're Russian
But you would certainly go there before trying your luck
with a fucking Pollock!

STEPHEN. Why are you so confident of that?
    How can you speak to that?

CALANTINI. For one very good reason I can speak to that
    Pollock is a *white* fish, whereas tuna is the darkest of Dark
    Meats
    You would go to Basses,

Giltheads and Breams,
You would try fucking Mackerel
Before you went for a Pollock
You would try all those other fish first

MARIANNE. Sorry… what is this 'Pollock'

CALANTINI. You know in the early years, when the fish first…
When the fish first went?
You remember all those old women?
Every couple of months an old woman would become an
overnight millionaire because she'd found some Breaded
Haddock in the bottom of a chest freezer
Do you recall to that?

They wordlessly confer. Into the microphone.

MARIANNE. We do

CALANTINI. Well at the time we just took it
We in the business, that is
We just took whatever we could get our hands on
As did the museums and cloning facilities and conservation
charities
We all panic-bought it and those old biddies made a killing

Beat.

But you see,
In the vast majority of cases this wasn't
'Atlantic Cod'
Or
'Fresh and Flaky Haddock'
In the main it was Breaded Pollock
Let me be clear

Into the mic.

ROY. Let the record show

Into the mic.

STEPHEN. Let the record show

CALANTINI. If you bought something that said 'Atlantic Cod'
or 'Fresh and Flaky Haddock'
And you bought the pure frozen flesh
No tampering
Then the chances are that it was the real deal
Cod or Haddock
But
If you bought it in breadcrumbs and it was being marketed to
you as 'white fish'
'White fish in breadcrumbs'
You were meant to *think*
'Atlantic Cod'
Or
'Fresh and Flaky Haddock'
Because of the association of the breadcrumbs
And, by extension, batter and other traditional methods of
preparation
But
In all likelihood,
It was, in fact, actually Pollock
The short-comings of the meat and of the flakeage being,
as they were, well-hidden under a breadcrumb coating or a
parsley Béchamel situation

Beat.

Point being
Pollock was the preeminent, go-to fall guy for the other *white
fish*
But *it would not have been a good fit*
By any stretch of the imagination
For
Dark
Oily
Sumptuous
…Sexy
Tuna fish

ROY. So it would have been obvious?

CALANTINI. If he had got his hands on a Pollock, it would
have been obvious

A schoolboy error

Beat.

A stupid schoolboy error

Beat.

The sort of error that only a dumb-fuck fuckin' schoolboy
would make

STEPHEN. Thank you

That analogy has been grasped

CALANTINI. Also

You *can* tuna, okay?

You *freeze* Pollock…

It would be a pretty incredible lapse in sanity for my brother
to think that he could seriously get away with cutting his
client's gear with some lumps of

Soggy,

Defrosted,

Breadcrumbed…

…Cat Slop

ROY. Cat Slop?

Into the mic.

CALANTINI. Cat Slop

MARIANNE. Expand on that

Speak to Cat Slop, briefly

CALANTINI. Cat Slop

Slop for cats

It's a Squibber's term

A Squibber being someone who makes Squib

It's a Squibber's term for bad Squib

Beat.

It is an insult to my brother's memory

We were many things but we were *never* petty crooks

MARIANNE *scoffs.*

MARIANNE. In fairness
    And with respect to the record, Mr Calantini
    That is exactly what you were

CALANTINI. No, no, no, no
    We were smugglers, bootleggers
    Dealers, for sure
    We *weren't* crooks

MARIANNE. Goodness me!
    Mr Calantini, you make it sound like you were some merry
    band of 'Jaunty Piraticals'
    You were mercenaries

CALANTINI. We were gourmands

MARIANNE. Poachers

CALANTINI. *Connoisseurs*

    MARIANNE *sneers*.

MARIANNE. Well I have to say, Mr Calantini, if nothing else
    It's heartening to see how well, despite some *rather dramatic
    shifts* in personal fortune, you've managed to maintain such a
    preposterously high level of self-regard

STEPHEN. You think very highly of your chosen profession
    don't you, Mr Calantini?

CALANTINI. Former profession, let the record show
    But yes,
    I did, as it happens, think that we were doing something
    worthwhile

MARIANNE. Worthwhile?!

CALANTINI. As it happens

MARIANNE. In what sense?
    In what sense 'worthwhile'?

CALANTINI. In the sense, I guess, that we made the world a
    better place

    Beat. MARIANNE *scoffs again*.

MARIANNE. Let the record show, Mr Calantini, that I am incredulous

She looks to her colleagues.

Let the record show that we are all three of us *completely* incredulous

Into the mic.

ROY. Let the record show

Into the mic.

STEPHEN. Let the record show that

CALANTINI. What can I say?
We enjoyed our lives and we helped others to enjoy theirs
We enabled them to have experiences that would have otherwise been denied them
I can't speak to what's wrong with that

MARIANNE. You can't speak to that?

CALANTINI. I *won't* speak to that
I won't expand on that
I won't *defend* that

STEPHEN. I wonder if Ivory Hunters tell themselves the same thing
Or Sex Traffickers
Or Drug Dealers

CALANTINI. Those aren't fair comparisons

MARIANNE. Oh, I think they are, Mr Calantini...
I think they are
I think *that they are*,
And
I intend to prove as much before we are finished here today

CALANTINI. *Good*

MARIANNE. Sorry
'Good'?

CALANTINI. Good...
    Good
    That's good, because right now, I have to say, this doesn't
    feel very useful
    This is a painful part of my life you're asking me about
    And I don't know why I'm here
    And, believe me, I *want* to feel useful
    Because I'm a private citizen who has served time for his
    crimes
    And who wants to give something back
    And who wants to feel useful
    But right now...

ROY. He doesn't feel useful

CALANTINI. I don't feel useful
    I feel punished

ROY. I can understand that, young man

STEPHEN. *Roy*

CALANTINI. This is all just very cruel
    And
    I don't know why
    I don't know why I am being punished
    Like this
    I don't know why I am being punished
    At all
    I have *been* punished!

MARIANNE. Oh I don't feel as though I need to punish you,
    Mr Calantini, I really don't
    And I am sorry that you feel that way
    Let the record show that

STEPHEN. Let the record show

MARIANNE. Because believe me
    Believe me when I say
    That I am quite sure that the guilt
    And
    The responsibility

And
The feelings that you feel
Presumably
For your brother's death
I feel that those feelings would most likely serve as
punishment enough

Pause.

CALANTINI. You're a cold bitch

Beat.

MARIANNE. Was there no sense of retribution when he died?
Of reckoning?

CALANTINI. Of course there was
I stopped doing what I had been doing, didn't I?

MARIANNE. Well...

CALANTINI. I stopped trading
If that's what you mean,
I stopped doing that

MARIANNE. Well that's up for speculation

CALANTINI. What does that *mean*?
I don't know what that means

MARIANNE. You will know what that means
Let the record show that we have other lines of inquiry first

STEPHEN. We will avail you of our meaning in due course, Mr
Calantini
Please be patient

Into the mic.

CALANTINI. That is becoming increasingly difficult!

Beat. Into the mic.

MARIANNE.... Noted, for the record
Please go on

Pause. Into the mic.

ROY. Please, sport

Beat.

CALANTINI. I wouldn't have continued
    Not after what happened to my brother

STEPHEN. And what did happen to him, Mr Calantini?
    What did they do, these men?
    These Russian men

Pause. CALANTINI is increasingly uncomfortable. Quietly.

CALANTINI. You know that they did to him

STEPHEN. Speak louder please

Beat. He does so.

CALANTINI. That information is in my court testimony from
    the criminal trial
    It was in the papers
    It was on the news
    You don't need me to speak to that here
    You don't need me to speak to that now

STEPHEN. Yes we do, Mr Calantini

ROY. For the sake of the record, sport

STEPHEN. For the sake of the record, Mr Calantini
    We do

Beat.

    What is said in this tribunal will, in years to come, be a
    matter of public record
    In short,
    Posterity is at stake
    And when future generations come to look back on this time
    When they come to learn of how we handled the
    extraordinary situation we now find ourselves in
    They will know that we did it right

MARIANNE. Let the record show

ROY. Let the record show

Beat.

STEPHEN. This tribunal has been convened in the hope of ascertaining whether or not the federal government of the United States should take out a suit of prosecution against you for the illegal handling of rare fish substances

CALANTINI. I have served my time for that and then some

STEPHEN. Yes!
For previous convictions, yes!

Beat.

You say that you stopped dealing after the murder of your brother
You say
That what happened to your brother meant that you could no longer continue
And that,
Thusly,
The allegations levelled against you now must be false

CALANTINI. I cannot speak to these allegations

MARIANNE. You cannot speak to them?

CALANTINI. I cannot speak to them because I don't know what they are!
I have no knowledge of these allegations
Let the record show that!

ROY. We will avail you of them, young man

STEPHEN. We will avail you of them, Mr Calantini

CALANTINI. Do that now please!

STEPHEN. Due process will be observed

CALANTINI. No!
Do that now!

Into the mics.

MARIANNE, ROY *and* STEPHEN. Due process must be observed

CALANTINI. I know my rights!

MARIANNE. Mr Calantini, enough!

Beat.

This is a private tribunal,
An informal inquest
If you are unhappy then you may leave any time
You are free to leave at any time

Pause.

CALANTINI. Fine

He gets up to leave.

MARIANNE. At which point, of course, you will be arrested for obstructing the course of this tribunal, and for obstructing the course of due process

STEPHEN. Due process shall be observed

MARIANNE. Due process *must* be observed!

Into his mic.

STEPHEN. Let the record show that due process *will* be observed
Let the record show

Pause. CALANTINI *returns to his microphone, leaning over the table and speaking into it. He does not yet sit. He may stand and walk around a bit more, agitated.*

CALANTINI. Let the record show this

Beat.

MARIANNE. Good

Beat. More shuffling, tension dissipated.

For the sake of our records, Mr Calantini,
For the sake of the *public* records,
And
So as better to maintain the integrity of our undertaking here today
Please expand on the events that caused you to renounce your former life

Please expand, for the benefit of this tribunal, on what the
Russians did to your brother

Pause. Away from the microphone.

CALANTINI. They 'Tinned' him

MARIANNE. Repeat that into the microphone please…

Pause. He leans over it as before.

CALANTINI. They *'Tinned'* him

*Pause. He moves away to the other end of the room, his voice
now totally unmediated by the mics.*

STEPHEN. To clarify
They 'Tinned' him?

CALANTINI. Yes
'Tinned'
We would say 'Canned'
It's an English thing
We say 'can of tuna'
They say 'tin of tuna'
As in 'tin can'
No one says that
No one says the whole thing
We say can
They say tin
And that's the word the Russians used
They 'Tinned' him

Pause.

ROY.…*Tinned*
Like one of your… squibs?
Like one of your tuna fish?

CALANTINI. Yeah
Exactly that
That is exactly the analogy that I would use
That is exactly the analogy that they were pursuing
That is exactly the analogy that *I believe* they were hoping to
generate

That they were hoping would *resonate* with me
It is that, exactly
That is how they 'Tinned' him
Like a tuna fish

Pause. CALANTINI, *still away from the mics, doubles over
and screams. Silence.*

ROY. Marianne?

MARIANNE. This tribunal will now observe a short
    I repeat
    A *short* recess

Music. Lights change. Time passes. Lights up. CALANTINI
is sat back at his desk.

Scene Three

CALANTINI. The black-market stuff,
    The dealing,
    The wild-fish market,
    Earlier you called it my profession, but it was more of a
    sideline

Beat.

We did it for the money, yes,
And
Admittedly
For the thrill of it
But
That wasn't our main line of work

Beat.

Our father was a leading marine biologist
And
A geneticist

When the fish went he quit his job at the university for a
private company
He had tenure there, but still, he told them to shove it
He didn't like being told what to do and so this new job, it
was freedom
And the money was great
And the resources that they made available to him
Were... well...
They were the sort of thing that he had been asking for, for
years

Pause.

But
As usual, in this sort of situation,
When the scales shift so rapidly
When the supply and demand matrix goes topsy-turvy
When that happens... the market goes into a frenzy

Beat.

When the fish went,
Because they went overnight
Demand didn't change
There was no 'steady decline'
There was no 'just getting used to it'
There were fish,
And then there weren't fish,
Simple as that
And so just because there were no fish
Because they went,
It didn't mean that people didn't keep wanting it
The fish I mean
They still wanted the fish
Fuck me, how they wanted it
Fuck me, how they fucking *craved* it
Fuck me, how they wanted more of it
More and more
More than... *ever*

Beat.

So the National Guard went in,
To supermarkets
And
To distribution centres
And
To processing plants
Seizing as much as it could of the existing supply
People calmed down
To an extent
But so then what?
People still wanted fish...
So they needed to make new fish,

Beat.

I will repeat that

Into the mic.

They needed to make new fish

MARIANNE. Is this significant?

STEPHEN. Is any of this significant?

CALANTINI. This is significant
All of this is significant

MARIANNE. Yes, well
See that it remains so

CALANTINI. You need to understand that idea
The idea that
'They needed to make new fish'
Because
It's a monstrous concept
And
A profound banality
And
It is indicative of a terrible greed

Beat.

STEPHEN. Right, but...

CALANTINI. Fuck the problems!
Fuck where the old fish went
They needed new ones
And they needed the information that was inside the old fish
That was inside the meat
Inside the *flakes*
The worlds of knowledge and meaning
That they perceived to be…
That they knew must reside…
In each fleck of Fish DNA
And so they pillaged the existing supply
They ripped through it
They churned through it
Like a fucking wood chipper
Can after can with no sense of restraint

Beat.

Oh
And fuck the fish that went that we weren't eating
By the way
Fuck Lionfish
Fuck Blowfish
Fuck Pufferfish
Fuck 'em!
Who gives a fuck about them?
We don't eat them
So we can't sell them
So we don't *miss* them

Beat.

So much waste
For so few answers

Pause.

MARIANNE. Your concern is touching, Mr Calantini
Your guilt is touching
But please
This much we know

Beat.

CALANTINI. Right

Pause.

ROY. In…um… the nicest possible way, Mr Calantini…

CALANTINI. In the nicest possible way?

ROY. In the nicest possible way
Please move now to the describing of
The 'Tinning'

CALANTINI. In the nicest possible way, I should move now to
describing the 'Tinning'?

ROY. Of your brother yes

STEPHEN. Please describe the 'Tinning' of your brother
And express to us how that experience was central to your
renouncing your involvement in the underground wild-fish
black-market
Please…

Pause.

CALANTINI. Somehow
Fuck knows how…
Suddenly people like my father
People who had been saying for years that something needed
to be done
And that there needed to be a mechanised response to
depleted fish stocks
Suddenly he is listened to
His theories are taken on board
Suddenly it's like…
Give a man a fish and feed him for a day
Teach a man to fish and feed him for a lifetime
But you know…
Teach a man to *grow his own* fucking fish
By the barrel load
And
Cheaply
And

Efficiently
And
In fucking test tubes…
And that man… He will give you the earth
And
The keys to the kingdom
And
He will pay you through the fucking nose
And then he will grow cruel
And impatient
As his coffers swell

STEPHEN. Is this relevant, Mr Calantini?

CALANTINI. YES OF COURSE IT'S FUCKING
RELEVANT!

Pause. He is standing. Pacing now.

But they don't taste right…

He picks up the microphone and intermittently holds it very close to his mouth for emphasis, picking up every breath.

They
Don't
Taste
Right
The *flakeage*
Is all wrong
The fish
Look like fish
…Mostly
And they move like fish
…Mostly
They can't *swim* exactly
And they'd be fucked in a current
But they can eat
And
Bob
And
Some of them have eyes

And
Most of them have mouths…
But it's just… *meat*
It's not *life*
It's not…
It's… closer, I think, to taking a cutting?
Like off of a tree, or a flower?
Do you know what I mean?

MARIANNE. Yes, you're attempting to construct a gardening
metaphor

CALANTINI. It's never quite the same, is what I mean
It's not the same… *thing* exactly
It's not what it was before
And of course they can't reproduce either…
Lots of them have got the right… bits,
Some of them in the right place,
But they wouldn't know what to do with them…
They have no instinct for it…
There's no sense of continuity
Of progeny
Like I said… it's just meat
Nasty, fleshy, quick-to-produce meat that tastes a bit like
something that nobody can really remember anyway

Beat.

That's where 'Squib' comes from
Something that has all the right bits in all the right places but
somehow fails to… 'go off'
If 'go off' could be termed a satisfying euphemism for sex
For ejaculation
Plus it's damp
Because it's fish…
Plus it sounds a bit like 'squid'…
So you know…
It's a little bit *fish* related

STEPHEN. Right, yes of course

CALANTINI. It all happened so quickly
    It sprung up overnight, the whole industry
    There wasn't time!
    There wasn't time to think of a good name!

STEPHEN. Yes, of course

CALANTINI. And everything grows so quickly, because it has
    to
    And so the profit margins start to collapse
    And
    The progress slows
    And
    The wages come down
    And
    Suddenly Dad isn't the 'wonder boy' any more
    And
    They start to treat him like shit
    And he doesn't like being treated like shit
    He was a clever man
    And
    He didn't suffer fools
    And
    He knows
    He knows in his heart that with a little more care
    And
    A little more time
    And
    A little more thought
    He could do it…
    He might not be able to make something that tasted like a
    Bluefin
    Or even a Yellowfin
    But he could at least get towards something that tasted like
    fish
    Like an actual fucking *fish*
    That *felt* like fish,
    That *felt* like it had been,
    In some way
    At some point,

Actually
Instinctively
Alive!

Beat.

He could maybe even get it,
To flake

Pause.

So he sets up on his own…
A cottage industry with smaller stocks, and smaller profits
An *artisanal* approach…
And by now he has two grown-up sons and so he puts us to
work…

Beat.

STEPHEN. Right

MARIANNE. Right…?

CALANTINI. And that…
    …*And that*

MARIANNE. Yes?

CALANTINI. Is the story
    Of how we ended up with the factory

*Pause. He drops the microphone back on the table and paces
again.*

STEPHEN. Great
    Brilliant
    That's fucking great

ROY. That is disappointing

MARIANNE. That is disappointing, Mr Calantini
    That was not the story we requested

CALANTINI. But it was

MARIANNE. It was not

CALANTINI. But it was

MARIANNE. But it was not!

CALANTINI. But it was,
Because…

MARIANNE. Because?
Because of what, Mr Calantini?!
Because of what?!

CALANTINI. Because *that* is *the* factory

MARIANNE. What is the factory?

CALANTINI. *That* is the factory

STEPHEN. That is the factory what?

CALANTINI. No!
No, no, not 'that is the factory what?'
'That is the factory… *where*?'

MARIANNE. Where?

CALANTINI. *Where*

ROY. Wait…
What?

MARIANNE. That is the factory where what, Mr Calantini?
That is the factory where what?

Pause. CALANTINI *goes to slump at the end of the table,
sitting on the floor, resting his back against the table leg,
perhaps obscured from the view of the audience. He takes
the microphone from the table and speaks into it, the sound
filling the space.*

CALANTINI. That is the factory where I was working late that
night
The factory where they brought my brother, after he
had apparently cut their priceless Yellowfin tuna with
bargain-basement Pollock

Beat.

They brought him back to his own factory
To our factory
To our father's factory
And that is where they 'Tinned' him

Pause, then softly into the mic.

STEPHEN. Speak to that, please

Still into the mic.

CALANTINI. I will speak to that

MARIANNE. Thank you

Still.

CALANTINI. I will

Into the mic.

ROY. Thank you for speaking to that

Pause.

CALANTINI. 'Tinned Him'
That is where they 'Tinned' him
Where they killed him,
And
Chunked him,
And
Put him into tins
Into cans
Into little tin cans
Like tuna fish

Beat.

MARIANNE. And they did that in front of you?
In your own factory?

CALANTINI. Yeah...
And actually they didn't chunk him, not to begin with,
The vast majority of him they cut into what they called
'steaks'

MARIANNE. Steaks?

CALANTINI. Yeah... anything that they considered to be a
coherent, self-contained area of flesh
A cheek would go in whole, that would be one can

A heart, that would be one can
A cylindrical cross-section of forearm or shin, that would be
one can
A clenched hand would, at a push, be one can

Beat.

Eventually there was just the scrag though,
Just bits of skin,
And
Testicle,
And
Cuticle
That's when they got the chunker out,
Not before

Pause, then loudly into the mic.

Let the record show that a 'chunker' is a machine that does
the chunking… if you were wondering

STEPHEN. Yes thank you… that bit, at least, was self-
explanatory

ROY. Goodness gracious…

Pause.

CALANTINI. So a trial went ahead and the Russians were all
executed
It was a traditional procedure, from what I know
Very respectful
Very calm
No undignified analogies or visual metaphors employed
Nothing…
Fishy

Beat.

There was, then, of course also a subsequent investigation
and I was jailed for the illegal procurement and trading of
wild-fish products
As you know, my sentence was commuted because I helped
the powers-that-be with their enquiries
But still

I think that most people would agree that
One way or another
I have served my time

Beat.

STEPHEN. Quite

Pause. Very close to his mic.

ROY. May God have mercy…
May God have mercy on their impoverished souls
Let the record show

Pause. The microphone is abandoned, as CALANTINI *gets up and holds court again.*

CALANTINI. And that is why it is ludicrous that I am here
And that is why I don't deserve to be hauled over the coals
by a fucking kangaroo court
And that is why I also think that most reasonable people
would believe me when I say that what I experienced that
night rather turned me off the prospect of future dealings in
that particular area

MARIANNE. Yes thank you, very good
That is significant
Let the record show that please

Synchronised into the microphone.

ROY *and* STEPHEN. Let the record show

CALANTINI. 'Let the record show!'
'Let the record show!'

Snatching his mic up from where it lies.

'LET THE RECORD SHOW!'

Pause.

Jesus
I mean
Jesus!
What kind of man do you take me for?
What kind of monster do you think I am?!

MARIANNE. That is as may be, Mr Calantini, but the *facts*
remain the same

CALANTINI. 'Facts'
What 'facts'
What fucking 'facts'
What fucking facts could possibly bear scrutiny against
that?!
What facts could bear the *weight* of that?
Expand on that!
Please!
Immediately!
Speak to that!
If you please!

Pause, THE SENATORS *look to each other and wordlessly
confer. It is time to proceed.*

MARIANNE. You accept that, as a man with previous
convictions for the illegal trading of wild-fish products,
it is only right that you be subject, as a condition of your
parole, to random screenings and warranted searches of your
property?

CALANTINI. I do

MARIANNE. And that, if found to be outside of the law again,
you should be subject to its full force?

CALANTINI. I do

MARIANNE. Then we have to take these developments
seriously

CALANTINI. What developments?!

STEPHEN. There have been developments,
Developments have come to light, via the circumstances of
your parole
Your parole agreement states that you should be subject to
random screenings and searches and a development has come
to light through the process of conducting one such random
screening and search

A development which gives us reason to believe that you are
once again stockpiling and trading in wild-fish products

CALANTINI. That's preposterous

MARIANNE. Is it?

CALANTINI. Yes

Away from the microphone.

MARIANNE. Roy, would you mind?

ROY. Not at all

ROY *removes an unmarked can from behind the bench and
places it on the desk in front of* CALANTINI. *He goes back
to his seat.*

MARIANNE. That can there,
The one in front of you,
Right there…
We found that at your factory
It's an old can,
And it's unlabelled

CALANTINI. I can up tonnes of squib every day
That can could have fallen off of the production line at any
point

MARIANNE. We have reason to believe that that isn't a can of
squib, Mr Calantini

Beat.

Do you remember, earlier in today's proceedings, when
my colleague here pressed you to describe in detail the
methodologies employed when ascertaining the contents of a
can without opening it?
X-rays, fluid retention, those tests, do you recall to that?

CALANTINI. I do

MARIANNE. Because we can have the record pulled if you
want to refresh yourself

CALANTINI. No, thank you
I recall to that
I recall to the discussion of those tests, yes

MARIANNE. Yes well
We have run tests of our own
Tests not unlike the ones that you so generously expounded upon for us, earlier

Beat.

Subsequently, we have reason to believe that this is a can of great significance
We have reason to believe that this is a can of pure, uncut, Southern Bluefin
Most likely from the Indian Ocean
Most likely a full steak
Most likely preserved in oil

Beat, then into the microphone.

ROY. This is significant

CALANTINI. Thank you, yes
I'm aware of that

Pause.

STEPHEN. Well?

CALANTINI. Well what?

STEPHEN. What do you have to say to that?

CALANTINI. I cannot speak to that

STEPHEN. You cannot speak to that?

Back looming over microphone.

CALANTINI. I cannot speak to that… because that is impossible
It is impossible for me to speak to something that is itself impossible

STEPHEN. Expand on that, please…

CALANTINI. There are only four cans of that calibre thought to be in existence

MARIANNE. Yes and we currently know the whereabouts of three of them

Reading from notes.

STEPHEN. One in China
One in the United Arab Emirates
One in the possession of a private citizen of great renown

CALANTINI. And you're seriously suggesting that this is the fourth?

MARIANNE. Yes. We have reason to believe that it might be

Pause.

CALANTINI. Well go on then,
Open it…
Let's take a fuckin' look

MARIANNE. Don't be so flippant

STEPHEN. You know we can't do that

CALANTINI. Why not?!

STEPHEN. You know why!

CALANTINI. No!
I *really* don't!

MARIANNE. Because we have to be sure of what we are opening before we open it

CALANTINI. Why?

Beat.

Why?

Beat, THE SENATORS *look at each other – 'are we really gonna do this thing?'*

What? So now none of you can tell me *why*?

MARIANNE. How did the fish... *go*, Mr Calantini?
Hmm?
You ever thought of that?
Ever thought of how they went?
Where they went?
Why they went?
That thought ever cross your selfish little mind?

CALANTINI. Well of course it did, but I don't see...

MARIANNE. How did the fish go?
Where did the fish go?
Why did the fish go?
The three great questions of our age

Beat.

And
Then
Also...
What did they know?
What did they see?
How did the sea make them feel?
How did what they saw make them feel?
Did they want to escape it?
Why did they want to escape it?
What did they want to escape?
Did they escape it?
How did they escape it?
Did they die?

Beat.

Do they know why they are gone?
Do they know where they are gone?
Do they know how they are gone?
Do they know that they are gone?
What does it mean that they are gone?
Does it mean something *to us* that they are gone?

Beat.

Is it a warning?
Is it a message?
Is it a sign?
Did they do it?
Or was it done to them?
If it was done to them, then who did the doing?
Did we do the doing?
What did we *do* if we did the doing?
What will they do to us in return?
Should we be ready for that?
Should we be scared?
Should we be prepared?
Should we make our peace with the lives that we've led?
Should we make our peace with the part that we've played?
Will they come back?
When will they come back?
How will they get back?
How can we help them to get back?
Should we help them to get back?
What have we lost in them?
What could we have learned from them?
How might we atone for them?
How might we appease them?
How might we help them?
All these questions
And chief amongst them
Where did they go?
How did they go?
Why did they go?

Beat.

Where did they go?
How did they go?
Why did they go?

Pause. She is lost in thought.

STEPHEN....Marianne?

She is jolted, immediately, back into the room.

MARIANNE. Do you know how AIDS works Mr Calantini?
Hmm?
How HIV works?

Beat.

CALANTINI....No

MARIANNE. You used a gardening metaphor earlier

Beat.

I'd like to use one too
I'd like to use one
For you now
It's like bindweed
For the human DNA helix
It curls itself around the stem like bindweed on a raspberry
cane
And it strangles it
And it becomes a part of it
Inextricable from it
And, slowly, it kills it
And it does this with information
With a special kind of 'living information'
A *'secret knowledge'* if you will
A secret knowledge that the body does not know
It kills it with what it does not know

Beat.

We want to know what we don't know, Mr Calantini
We want to know what the fish didn't know
If they didn't know it
But to do that we have to find the bindweed
We have to find an intact vine
We have to find the thing that made the fish go
And we happen to think that it might be attached to the fish
itself
Like a sort of
Fish
AIDS

CALANTINI. Pure fantasy

Suddenly ferocious.

MARIANNE. MR CALANTINI, I'M SPEAKING

Beat.

I'M SPEAKING

Beat, and then very calm again.

We know,
Or at least, we *think* we know,
That the Southern Bluefin has,
Locked in its DNA,
Coiled around it,
Like a virus,
Like Fish AIDS,
This 'secret knowledge' of why the fish went…

Beat.

But, as soon as you open the can
As soon as you let air in
It starts to degrade
The secrets start to… *trickle* out
And so we need to be sure
So that we can be prepared
So that we can *be sure*
So that we can then take steps
Make audits
And
Appraisals
And
I guess…

Beat, she thinks.

I guess…
Come to know whether or not we know what we need to
know about knowing things about fish
To know that opening this can,
Now,

At this point,
Would be more worthwhile than it would be not to open it...
yet...
Does that make sense?

Into the microphone.

CALANTINI. No
    ...No, and all of this is insane

ROY. It is not insane

CALANTINI. It is insane and, God willing, the record will
    show that to be the case

MARIANNE. Earlier on in these proceedings you decried the
    wasteful and reckless actions of previous generations towards
    our remaining wild-fish stock
    As someone who used to make a living,
    An obscene and disgusting living,
    Off of the sale and subsequent consumption of contraband
    wild fish
    I find that shift in your sentiments to be admirable

Right into the mic.

CALANTINI. Thank you

MARIANNE. But your demonstrated compassion
    And
    Your apparent scepticism with regards to both what this can
    contains and what might be gained by studying its contents,
    That does not now put you above suspicion

Beat.

We have reason to believe that
As someone with your expertise
And with your background
There is every reason to suggest that you know very well the
contents of this unmarked can
And
That you have procured it illegally for the purpose of either
private resale or private consumption

Such transactions are banned under United States Federal
Law, Mr Calantini, as you well know
You must tell us now if that is the case
For the sake of the secret knowledge
For the sake of our sacred task
We will be lenient

Pause.

CALANTINI. You're fucking kidding me

MARIANNE. There is no need to incriminate anyone
Your father could have procured it before the Federal ban
Before we realised our mistakes
Before we curtailed our reckless ways

CALANTINI. I told you, I don't know anything

STEPHEN. We're offering you a way out here, Mr Calantini
Tell us what we need to know
If you know it
And we will be lenient when public prosecution follows
I promise
Tell us it's Blue, and we will take the can, and we will be
lenient

Into the mic.

MARIANNE. We will let you go free

Beat, ROY *and* STEPHEN *look at her with surprise.*

You understand our predicament. You have spoken to it
yourself
Only when the fish went did people want to protect fish
Only when the fish went did we desire to make new fish
And the money
And the energy
And the focus
That came after the event
We need to recapture that now
We need to harness it and use it for good

Beat.

Only if we know that this is Blue can we proceed
Only if we know that this is Blue can we hope to harness the
money
And
The Energy
And
The Focus
That the exercise demands
People will want to know the secrets that the Bluefin Tuna
holds
But only if they can be sure
In advance
Of the validity of the enterprise

Beat.

We would open it in controlled conditions
We would give it the best care

ROY. Because we would know what colour its fins are

MARIANNE. And then we would use it
All of it
Shred
By
Tiny
Shred

Very close to the mic.

ROY. Flake
By
Scrumptious flake

MARIANNE. And we would try and ascertain where they went
And what went wrong
And maybe
God willing
How we might get them back

Beat.

How we might make them again

How we might make the great empty blueness *teem* again
How we might make the world anew again
In your father's image
Doesn't that sound like the sort of thing that he would like?
Doesn't that sound like the sort of thing that he would be in
favour of?

CALANTINI. How *fuckin'* dare you?

He goes to leave. He is away from the mic again.

MARIANNE. Mr Calantini

CALANTINI. I will leave you
With nothing

He goes to leave.

MARIANNE. I don't think you're going to do that, Mr Calantini

CALANTINI. Oh yeah?
Why not?

MARIANNE. Because I think you want to know
Because I think you want to know, too

Beat.

Don't you want to know why they went, Mr Calantini?
Doesn't that interest you?
Wouldn't that have interested your father?

There is a long pause. MARIANNE *is standing now, looming
over the desk. Eventually* CALANTINI *goes over to her. Not
looking at her, he snatches her microphone from the desk and
speaks closely but quietly into it.*

CALANTINI. Excuse me

He leaves, bursting out through the double doors.

MARIANNE. There will be no recess at this time
Mr Calantini!
Stay where you are!
There will be no recess at this time!

She stands, imperious, looking towards the door for a long time. Eventually ROY, *after much wordless conference with* STEPHEN, *breaks the silence.*

ROY. Marianne?

MARIANNE. There will be a recess of an undetermined
        duration at this time
        Let the record show that

Beat. She slams the table.

Fuck!

Lights, music.

ACT TWO

Scene One

ROY *and* STEPHEN *are relaxed, slightly.* ROY *remains seated whilst* STEPHEN *prowls.* MARIANNE *remains focused on the door. She is up and pacing and smoking.*

ROY. You know you can't do that in here, right?

MARIANNE. Fuck off, Roy

Silence.

STEPHEN. Since when did you smoke, anyway?

MARIANNE. Since I started jogging

STEPHEN. Jogging?

MARIANNE. Yeah, jogging
Y'know, like purposeful running?

STEPHEN. Yeah
I know what jogging is

MARIANNE. Then why ask it, Stephen?
Why ask 'jogging?', in a questioning tone, if you know what jogging is?

STEPHEN. I meant to question the relevance of that
In relation to your smoking, I mean

MARIANNE. ...Right
Sure

STEPHEN. Like,
What does your jogging...
What does your *starting to jog*
Have to do with your starting to smoke?

She thinks and shrugs.

MARIANNE.…I guess I had to do something to balance it out

Silence.

ROY. Y'know… I do miss the English

MARIANNE. Jesus
He's back on the English, Stephen

ROY. No
No, I do

MARIANNE. Check it's water in his glass this time, will yah?

STEPHEN *smirks*.

ROY. I miss their… *irony*
You know?
Their… *dry wit*

Beat.

And the Dutch, I miss them too

STEPHEN. The Dutch aren't gone

ROY. Yeah, I know
I know that
But I miss their tulips
All those beautiful tulips
I'd swap the Dutch out for their tulips any day

STEPHEN. Yeah well, shit happens
Whaddaya gonna do?

MARIANNE. That's awfully cynical

STEPHEN. The land was too flat, enough said
The land was too flat and so they had to go

Beat.

The tulips that is
Not the Dutch

MARIANNE. No, not the Dutch
The Dutch survived
God knows how, but they did

ROY. Their houses floated and so they lived
    I reckon that's about the sum of it

STEPHEN. Right

ROY. The English...
    Didn't float
    They didn't build the new houses and so they didn't float

    Beat.

    The English...
    I think...
    Were too afraid of change

STEPHEN. Adapt or die, I guess

MARIANNE. Jesus, you're a cold piece of shit, you know that?

STEPHEN. Yeah?

MARIANNE. Yeah

STEPHEN. Yeah, well it takes one to know one
    People in glass houses, Marianne

    Beat.

    Actually, you know what? Give me one of those

    Meaning the cigarettes, he goes towards MARIANNE *who backs away.*

MARIANNE. Fuck off
    Get your own

STEPHEN. Oh, come on!

    He moves again.

MARIANNE. I mean it, get fucked. I need these
    They're medicinal

STEPHEN. Oh yeah, like fuck they are

MARIANNE. They are, they're for my headaches

    Silence.

    I get such terrible fucking headaches these days, you
    wouldn't believe

Headaches and Night Terrors
And lesions and cysts
Still
…That's the menopause, I guess

She smokes, A long silence.

ROY. Y'know, I went to *Norfolk* once
In England

MARIANNE. Actually, Roy, you know what? Maybe we can
just have five minutes, okay?
Five minutes of peace, maybe?

Beat.

ROY. Norfolk was in England
I went there

MARIANNE.…Okay

ROY. As a very little boy, I went
And
Even as a very little boy I *liked* the English
I liked their… *irony*, even then
Without really knowing what it was
You could read it in their smiles

STEPHEN. Oh yeah…
Their monstrous smiles

ROY. No
No
That was a common misconception
Their smiles were fine
Their smiles were quite beautiful, actually, in their way
In their way they were quite… magnificent

Beat.

Every mouth a cave
Brimming with ancient-seeming stalagmites of blemished
ivory

Beat.

I adored it
England
Norfolk
I adored their tulips

MARIANNE. *Jesus, Roy*
That was the Dutch
The Dutch had the tulips

To STEPHEN.

He's confusing himself again

ROY. No
No
The English had them too

Beat.

Because it was very flat, Norfolk
Like Holland was
Flat
And
Long
And
The sea was a long way away

Beat.

The sea was so far away from the land
From the rest of the beach
And
I was a tiny kid at the time
And
I couldn't walk as far as the sea
And
I remember thinking how painful that must have been
For the English
For the English people of Norfolk
Because the English loved the sea
And so…
And so to be so *close* to it
And to hear its sounds

And to live a life which is marked by its secrets and rhythms
But to not be able to *reach* it
That must have been so painful for them
Not to have been able to reach *their* sea

Beat.

And then eventually, of course, it reached them

Beat.

An irony that would not have been lost on them
Had they not become so hopelessly lost themselves

Silence.

I remember…

MARIANNE. *Jesus*

ROY. I remember I went to a Norfolk church in Norfolk
I was *drawn* there
I was
Drawn *in*
Because there was music playing
Beautiful and arresting and alluring sounds

Beat.

'A Norfolk Symphony'
It was called
Or something
Something like that
And
It was written by a man who had been there
And
Loved it
And
Loved its light
And
Its big skies
And
Put that love and that light and that bigness into his music

Beat.

It was my father who told me that
Because that was the kind of thing that he knew
And
I remember
He held my hand as I listened in that church
And
As I cried
As I cried…

Beat.

… As I cried the tears of a little boy who was
Calm
In
An *adult* way
For the first time in his life

Beat.

Calm in an adult way
Calmed
Becalmed
In
An adult way
By
Art
By
Listening
And
As I was listening to that beautiful music
In that beautiful place that we've lost
I felt suddenly full of the Wisdoms of the Past
In a way that was special and secret and new

He inexpertly hums one of the more hummable bits of Ralph Vaughan Williams' 'Norfolk Rhapsody No. 1' and then misremembers, tries again, fails and falls silent. Silence.

STEPHEN. Do you think he knows?

MARIANNE. No
But I hope he lies
I hope he tells us what we want to hear so that we can get that fucking thing open

STEPHEN. What makes you so sure he's coming back?

MARIANNE. Oh he's coming back
He's coming back, alright. Men like that
Are
Addicted to pain

Silence. ROY *hums again.*

Shut up, Roy!

ROY. Sorry, Marianne

Silence.

STEPHEN. When I worked at the CIA we used to just torture people
All the time

MARIANNE. Yeah?

STEPHEN. Oh yeah
We weren't supposed to but we did

Beat.

People say that information gained under torture is inaccurate, but that all depends on the metric by which it's being measured
It's absolutely true that the *quality* of the information you manage to accrue is questionable
But the *quantity*
My God, the sheer *wealth* of… *stuff…*
Of *shit* that you can get people to say
That has a *truth* to it which is all of its own

Beat.

All we'd need is a pan of boiling sugar
And we could get him to say whatever we want

Beat. MARIANNE, *amused, hands* STEPHEN *a cigarette.*

MARIANNE. Here
…Freak

He lights it and they smoke, silence.

Suddenly there is a banging on the fire door. THE
SENATORS *look round to see where it is coming from.*

ROY. What, in God's name, is that?

STEPHEN. It's knocking, Roy
Someone is knocking on the fire door

From the other side of the door.

CALANTINI. It's me!
Let me in
It's me!

THE SENATORS *look at each other, alarmed.*

MARIANNE. I beg your pardon?

CALANTINI. The door doesn't open from this side, let me in

STEPHEN *goes over to the door.*

STEPHEN. Umm
That's a fire door, Mr Calantini

CALANTINI. Yeah…

Beat.

I can't open it

MARIANNE. Oh for God's sake

STEPHEN. Well
Come round
Come back through the main entrance

Beat.

CALANTINI. No…
No, just open this door, please

STEPHEN. That's a fire door

CALANTINI. Yeah
I know

STEPHEN *looks at* MARIANNE *for guidance. She shrugs.*

STEPHEN. I might trigger an alarm if I open it
Go round

Pause.

CALANTINI....No

MARIANNE. *Jesus fucking Christ*

CALANTINI. No, I can't do that

STEPHEN. Mr Calantini
Stop horsing around

MARIANNE. Just open the door for him, Stephen

STEPHEN. But...

MARIANNE. Just...
Please

STEPHEN *opens the fire door.* CALANTINI *re-enters with a harpoon gun.*

CALANTINI. Thanks
I didn't think they'd let me put this through the metal
detectors out front

MARIANNE. Oh my God!

CALANTINI. This is a government building after all

STEPHEN. Jesus!

STEPHEN *makes a break for the double doors.* CALANTINI
calmly levels the harpoon at him.

CALANTINI. Stay where you are, please

He stops dead.

MARIANNE. Jesus

ROY. What the fuck even is that thing?!

CALANTINI. After the Russians
After I testified
I started carrying my dad's old harpoon gun with me, in my
car

STEPHEN. Why?

CALANTINI. I thought it might come in useful

STEPHEN. Right…

CALANTINI. Yeah

STEPHEN. Why?
How?
What do you plan to do with it?

CALANTINI. You'll see

MARIANNE. Roy

ROY. Yeah…

MARIANNE. Under the desk
Under my place at the desk
There is a small button
Can you see that?
On the underside of the desk
Can you see it?

ROY. Yeah

MARIANNE. It's a panic button
Press it
Press it and the police or the Secret Service or someone will come

CALANTINI. Don't do that

He gestures the harpoon gun in ROY'*s direction.*

That is unnecessary

MARIANNE. Unnecessary?!
I have reason to believe that you're going to shoot us, Mr Calantini

CALANTINI. If I had wanted to do that then I would have brought a gun
This piece of shit is an antique
It takes, like, five minutes to reload, or something, at least
That's not why I brought it in here

MARIANNE. Well then why did you bring it?

CALANTINI. Leverage

Beat.

You

Meaning ROY.

Move away from the button
And you

Meaning STEPHEN.

Get away from that door
Come and stand by *madam* here

They do so. Pause.

MARIANNE. Well?

CALANTINI. I want the recording equipment turned off
I want what I'm about to tell you to be off the record so they
need to be turned off

MARIANNE. No, no, no you can't
You can't do that. It has to stay on the record
To have any jurisdictional relevance whatsoever, Mr
Calantini, the record must show

Quietly.

STEPHEN *and* ROY. *The record must show*

CALANTINI. But I don't want it to have jurisdictional
relevance
I don't give a shit about jurisdictional relevance
I just want to talk to you
Just you three

MARIANNE *starts to laugh.*

What?
What's so funny?

MARIANNE. Oh
      I'm sorry, I really am
      But…
      I am *not* interested

      Beat.

      This may surprise you, Mr Calantini, and I am sorry if it
      presents as rudeness
      But I am not interested
      Personally speaking
      In what you have to say, okay?

CALANTINI. I don't believe that to be true

MARIANNE. It is the truth

CALANTINI. It is not
      I can see that it is not
      In your eyes
      I can see it
      And I will prove it

MARIANNE. Then prove it

CALANTINI. Then turn the microphones off

MARIANNE. No

      Pause, they stare each other down.

CALANTINI. It's a simple thing
      The can
      It's a profoundly simple technology

      Beat.

      The design is French in origin, but it was made popular
      Like a lot of things
      By the English
      By their Empire
      They gave cans to their soldiers on long expeditions so as to
      help keep their food rations fresh

      Beat.

Since the time of Napoleon, they were doing that
And
Like…
Nelson
And
The Iron Duke of Wellington

Beat.

This, by the way, is a really, *really* long time for a technology
to have stayed relevant
But it has
Because it works

Beat.

In the mass-marketisation of wild-fish products the can
superseded, in popularity, all known pre-existing methods of
preservation
Oil preserves fish
And
Brine preserves it for slightly longer still
But you don't need either of those ingredients when you start
sealing your fish in cans

Beat.

They still added them in, of course
Oil and brine, that is
Out of respect for tradition
And
In deference to style and sentiment
But it's completely redundant, really
Once the fish is in a can
Because, you see

Beat. He climbs up onto the table.

There really is no substitute for it, actually
There really is no substitute
In the pursuit of freshness
To keeping your fish

Beat, he levels the harpoon gun at the can.

…Airtight

STEPHEN. No!

MARIANNE. No don't!

CALANTINI. Turn the microphones off

MARIANNE. Okay! Okay!

CALANTINI. One of you does it
　　The other two stay still

MARIANNE. Okay
　　Roy?

ROY. Yeah?

MARIANNE. Do you know how to do it?

ROY. What?

MARIANNE. Do you know how to turn the recorders off?

ROY. What?
　　No!

MARIANNE. No you don't
　　Or no you won't?

ROY. No, I won't!

MARIANNE. Ah Jesus

ROY. That's probably a fucking felony or something

MARIANNE. Stephen?

STEPHEN. We don't have your… uh… *authority*, Marianne
　　This needs some authority behind it

MARIANNE. Oh for God's sake
　　You spineless fucks!

ROY. I don't see, if we want the damn thing open anyways, why
　　we don't just let him open it

CALANTINI. Sure thing!

STEPHEN. No!

MARIANNE. NO!
    No, we're not ready yet
    We don't know enough yet!
    If we open it now then we could lose what we want to know,
    so no
    Fine
    I will do it
    Me
    I will do it
    I'm going to go and do it okay?
    I'm going to go behind the desk

CALANTINI. Sure

MARIANNE. Okay?

CALANTINI. Okay, sure

    She does this. From behind the desk.

MARIANNE. Okay…
    Okay I've done that

CALANTINI. Okay

    CALANTINI *taps one of the mics to make sure. He sighs a
    long sigh.* MARIANNE *comes back round.*

STEPHEN. Mr Calantini…
    Please
    What's this all about?

    Pause, he thinks.

CALANTINI. I think you should know that
    You're wasting your time

    Beat.

    Now, I know that isn't what you want to hear
    And
    I know that isn't what you need to hear
    And so you're probably not gonna listen
    But it's the truth, all the same
    The truth is that the truth you're looking for…

Looking for that truth
That's a waste of time

Beat.

ROY. So it's not
…Bluefin?

Quietly.

STEPHEN. Oh God

CALANTINI. No, no it is
More likely than not, it is

MARIANNE. Oh, thank Christ

CALANTINI. If the data you've collected is correct, that is
And if it has been correctly read

MARIANNE. Thank Christ, thank God

CALANTINI. But that won't help you, is my point
That isn't meaningful
I'm afraid

Beat.

But you won't accept that, you see, because you won't accept
what I'm about to tell you, and so don't worry
In a minute we can turn the microphones back on and I will
say what needs to be said for the sake of the record

MARIANNE. For the sake of the record, yes
For the sake of the record

CALANTINI. And you can get your money and your time and
your resources
And you can find out for yourselves
And you can lose your hope slowly
In a slow trickle of hopelessness on a human scale
Because that is the only way that humans learn, isn't it?
Slowly
And with great effort
And with greatening pain

And only after it is all too late
And I will let you do that
I will
But first I have to tell you some things
Just you

Beat.

Things that I don't want to be heard by anyone else
Things that, unfortunately, make a very strong case for our
hopelessness as a species
And
Because humans don't like that and they react against that
And because they hope against hope and they believe what
they want to believe
They will choose to hear only the facts of *how* I know the
things that I know
And those facts will cause rage
And rancour
And hatred and shame
And I have already had quite enough of that, thank you very,
very much

MARIANNE. How do you know this?

CALANTINI. Because humans are failed and broken things
    Because humans are squibs

MARIANNE. No, no
    I don't mean about humans
    About their frailties and their failures
    I mean about the Bluefin
    How do you know that the answers we seek
    Aren't in that can?

CALANTINI. Because my father told me

MARIANNE. And how did he know?

CALANTINI. Because it was his job to know

MARIANNE. And why didn't he tell anybody else?

CALANTINI. Because what good could that *possibly* have
done?

Beat.

Between tendering his resignation and starting his own
company, my father took a vacation
A nice long one
All over the world
He went all over the world but he wasn't just 'travelling', oh
no
He was surreptitiously buying up supplies of extremely rare
wild-fish product

Beat.

He was buying Bluefin

MARIANNE. *What?*

CALANTINI. This was before the ban, you see
    This was before there was even an idea of a ban
    But he did it because he anticipated that, because of its rarity
    and its primacy,
    The Bluefin could start to work a hopeful magic in the hearts
    of man
    And he did it because he knew that those hopes would be
    misplaced

Beat.

He knew the hope that the Bluefin might hold some kind of
key
Some kind of 'secret knowledge' as to why the fish went
He knew that would be based on nothing more than the
heightened sensibility, which resides within every broken
human soul, towards the making of great myths
Myths of Salvation
Myths of Redemption
Myths of Deliverance and of Restoration

Beat.

He knew that those theories would come
And that they would be baseless
And so he went and bought it
All of it
As much as he could get his hands on

ROY. Why?

CALANTINI. Why?

MARIANNE. Yes, why?

CALANTINI. Why, so that we could eat it, of course

Beat.

MARIANNE. Jesus Christ

CALANTINI. We lived off of it
For weeks

MARIANNE. *Jesus Christ*

CALANTINI. Months
Years
Held some back
Opened it on special occasions
Fetishised it
Ritualised it
Made it special
Made it uniquely *ours*

ROY. How could you?

STEPHEN. Why did he do that?

CALANTINI. He did it so as to *rarefy* the Bluefin
So as to make it as unattainable as possible and to make
searching for it hard
And fraught
He did it so as to put it beyond reach
And to keep the mystery alive

MARIANNE. What mystery?

CALANTINI. The mystery of, as you put it, 'the secret
knowledge'
The hysterical notion that there might be something worth
finding
He felt that that would most likely be important

MARIANNE. Why?
Why was that important?

CALANTINI. Because it stopped us all from feeling forced to
do what he did
It stopped us from having to look *inside of ourselves* for the
answer
It stopped us all from feeling forced to confront the most
awful of truths about ourselves

MARIANNE. Which is what, exactly?

CALANTINI. Which is that we're fucked

Beat.

And that we're fucked because we fucked up
And that we fucked up because *we're* fucked up
And that we did this
And that we are doing this
And that we can't be stopped
And that this *whole thing* isn't the *end* of a thing but rather
the *beginning* of a bigger thing
And that this thing, *that is a thing*, is a thing that will most
likely end with the end of us
And
I don't know why
But
I happen to think that maybe that is why they went
That seems to me to be as good a reason as any
That seems to me to be as good a reason as any to tell our
grandkids
That 'there were these things that we called fish and that they
went because we made them'
I guess...
I guess... that's as good a thing to tell them as any

Pause.

MARIANNE. Jesus Christ
    That's…
    What can we do with that?!

CALANTINI. What you will
    It's the truth of the matter at any rate

She thinks very hard.

MARIANNE. Well
    I think
    That
    It's a bullshit truth

CALANTINI. It's not

MARIANNE. I think it's *your* truth and nothing else
    And I reject it
    I reject your bullshit truth, you fucker
    Do you hear me?
    I reject it!
    You fucker!

STEPHEN. What the fuck are we supposed to do now?

To CALANTINI.

ROY. What does it taste like?

MARIANNE. Roy!

To STEPHEN.

Nothing
We do exactly as planned

To ROY.

CALANTINI. Like life
    Like the purest *essence* of life

To MARIANNE.

STEPHEN. How can we?
    How can we just go on as planned?!

To CALANTINI.

ROY. Oh, that sounds wonderful
     You're so lucky

     To STEPHEN.

MARIANNE. Because we have to!
     That's how

     To ROY.

CALANTINI. Yeah
     I know…

     Pause.

MARIANNE. No
     It's bullshit
     We keep going

CALANTINI. That's fine
     You do what you think is best

MARIANNE. And you!
     As for you
     You fucker!
     They're going to hang for this
     They will fucking hang you for this
     For what you've done
     You fucking cunt!
     They will string you up from the Washington Monument for
     what you've done!

CALANTINI. And what have I done?

MARIANNE. Gorged yourself!
     Like a fucking animal!
     Consumed…
     The future
     Consumed it on a grotesque scale
     Eating away at any hope we had of finding out what went
     wrong

CALANTINI. You know what went wrong
     Deep down you know it

    The Bluefin is just a fish!
    Just like any other fish!
    IT'S JUST
    A FUCKING
    FISH!

MARIANNE. We keep going with the project
    We stay the course
    We keep going

STEPHEN. What?!

MARIANNE. This isn't on the record
    This whole thing, Stephen… it isn't on the record
    And *he* wants to keep it *off* of the record as much as anyone,
    right?

CALANTINI. Right

MARIANNE. Right?
    Right
    So there
    No one needs to know
    Nobody needs to hear his crazy bullshit
    He gets off scot free
    His father's reputation remains intact
    And we still get to do what is *necessary*
    It is Bluefin after all!
    He said as much!

STEPHEN. But there's nothing there!

MARIANNE. According to who?
    To him!
    And his fucker father
    His fucking father who was fucking demented for all we
    know

ROY. Did you sell it?
    Or just eat it?

MARIANNE. Roy, please!

CALANTINI. We just ate it, man

ROY. *That's amazing*

MARIANNE. Roy, I am begging you!
    Please just…

STEPHEN. Forget it, Marianne!
    It's over
    Okay?
    He must have been sure
    The man was probably a genius or something
    Right?

CALANTINI. He was

STEPHEN. See?!

MARIANNE. Says who?
    This dumbass fucktard?!

ROY. Do you have any left?

MARIANNE. *Roy,* I swear to God!

CALANTINI. After my brother and my father died I stopped
    eating it altogether

MARIANNE. Can we focus?!

STEPHEN. Hang on Marianne

MARIANNE. We don't have time for this!

ROY. So you do have some left?

CALANTINI. Sure

MARIANNE. Oh for fuck's sake!

    STEPHEN *is thinking.*

STEPHEN. Wait
    Hang on, Marianne
    Wait

MARIANNE. *Stephen…*

STEPHEN. Wait!

    Beat.

    How much?
    How much do you have left?

    CALANTINI *thinks, does some mental maths and then*
    shrugs.

CALANTINI. Fifty…
Seventy cans

Beat.

STEPHEN. Jesus

MARIANNE. Jesus fucking Christ

STEPHEN *is thinking again.*

ROY. That's… *amazing*

MARIANNE. Well that's just fucking spectacular
So now we have seventy cans of Bluefin tuna that we can't
use
That's we can't *seize*
Without people knowing about it
And we can't have people knowing about it
Without telling them *why* the cans exist
And we can't tell them why the cans exist without telling
them why his supposedly genius father, or whatever, went
and collected them all in the first place

Beat.

I mean… for instance, where are they?
These cans?
Where are they right now?

CALANTINI. In my basement

MARIANNE. Right
Exactly
I mean…
Why would they be in his basement?
It doesn't make the slightest sense
What reason could we possible give?

CALANTINI. Tell them the truth!
'They're there because they're meaningless'

MARIANNE. Shut your mouth!

STEPHEN *is really thinking hard now.*

STEPHEN. It doesn't matter

MARIANNE. Oh, please
    'It doesn't matter'
    Of course it matters Stephen!

ROY. I think we should keep them.

MARIANNE. Roy…

ROY. Share them out and eat them

MARIANNE. Roy, will you shut the fuck up?!

ROY. Why?
    What difference does it make?

CALANTINI. Exactly…

MARIANNE. We need them!
    We need all of them for the
    For the…
    For the…
    For the research!
    So we can figure this thing out!

CALANTINI. There's nothing to figure out

STEPHEN. You're missing the point

MARIANNE. Oh am I?
    Oh thank you, Stephen

CALANTINI. There is no problem
    For you
    To solve!

STEPHEN. Exactly!
    Marianne, there is nothing we can do

    Beat.

MARIANNE. And that's your winning analysis is it, Stephen?
    Brilliant

STEPHEN. But…

MARIANNE. Brilliant!

STEPHEN. But!
More than that!

Beat.

Look…
We can't knowingly leave those cans there
We can't keep it a secret
But
There is no actual reason why we should
Because there is nothing in that can
Or any of the cans
That can help us

MARIANNE. You don't know!

STEPHEN. But!
But!
We go on record
We say again what he just said to us
We get those cans
And we use them
We use them all
For research into cloning
And into genetics
And
Reproduction
And
Maybe
Maybe from that we can build something
A new fish
Like… a new flagship fish
Like… a new Bluefin
Something that we can put back into the sea

Beat.

If we know more than we know now then maybe
Maybe we can start anew again
And that way

That way…
Maybe we can start to put things right again

Pause.

MARIANNE. Right…
    Yeah…

STEPHEN. Seventy cans, Marianne!
    Seventy cans is a research programme
    Seventy cans is a government initiative
    Seventy cans is a massive fuck-off lab
    And
    A team of top research scientists!
    Think of the jobs that would be created

MARIANNE. Right

STEPHEN. And the money that could be made
    …The money that *we* could make

CALANTINI. What?

STEPHEN. And the fame
    And the success
    Think of the opportunity this could be!
    For us!
    We'd be like
    Founding Fathers
    And Mothers
    Or something

CALANTINI. *Jesus Christ…*

STEPHEN. What?
    This is an opportunity
    Marianne, listen to me
    This is an opportunity
    We put him on trial
    We seize his assets
    We change the world
    We could be President, Marianne
    We could all be President!
    Even Roy…

ROY. Thank you for that, Stephen

MARIANNE. Even Roy?

STEPHEN.... Yes
Even
Roy

Beat.

President Roy
President Stephen
President Marianne
Now, does that not have a ring to it?

CALANTINI. FUCK!
FUUUUUUUUUUCK!

MARIANNE. Jesus Christ!

ROY. Holy smokes!

CALANTINI. You don't learn do you?!
You don't get it?
You fuckers…
You never fucking learn, do you?
Fuckers never fucking learn!

*He takes his harpoon gun and, holding it like a spear brings
it above the can on the table.*

MARIANNE. No!

He brings it down, piercing the can. Pause.

…Jesus
Jesus Christ

CALANTINI. Tick tock… Fuckers

MARIANNE. Oh my God!
Oh my God!
We need…

STEPHEN. It doesn't matter

MARIANNE. We need to get help
We need to call the police or something
Stephen
We need…

STEPHEN. It doesn't matter!
Remember?
There are seventy cans now
That can is not *the* can
That can doesn't matter!

MARIANNE. Yes but, Stephen

STEPHEN. Marianne…

MARIANNE. Yes but, Stephen
What we need
What we *need*
That could be in there!
Shit!
Shit!
We're losing it!
We're losing it!

STEPHEN. Losing what?
Losing What?
Marianne
Marianne, look at me
Look at me!
Losing what?
There's nothing to find

MARIANNE. Right but…
But…
He's opened the can, Stephen
Seventy isn't infinity, Stephen
Seventy isn't an infinite supply
We need
We need… every can
We need every shard, every flake
And
And

And
Oh God
Oh God!
It's like it's happening again…
I feel sick!

STEPHEN. Marianne…

MARIANNE. It's like we're doing all the wrong things all over
again
All that wastefulness!
The
The
The wastefulness!
The wastefulness! It hurts my heart, Stephen!
It
It
It hurts my heart!

STEPHEN. Okay
Okay!

MARIANNE. We need to go and find help
Okay?
Okay?!

STEPHEN. Okay
Okay
Stay calm
Okay?

To CALANTINI.

You're for it now, buddy!
What you just did was a federal offence
Let the record show!
Roy, you stay here okay?

MARIANNE. Make sure he doesn't do any more damage, Roy

ROY. Oh so *now* you trust me?!

MARIANNE. Enough!
Just make sure!
Okay?

ROY. Alright
   Fine
   Jesus

MARIANNE. Alright
   Alright
   We'll be back…
   Jesus Christ

STEPHEN. Be calm!

MARIANNE. I'm calm
   I'm calm

   To CALANTINI.

   We'll be back you fucker

   Whilst exiting out through the double doors.

   You fucking fucker!

   STEPHEN *lingers. There is a moment of stillness and quiet.*

STEPHEN. I know you think I'm just some dumb-fuck
   politician
   Some dumb-fuck suit, too worried about his vote-share to
   truly rock the boat
   But you don't get into a room like this
   You don't get to *be*
   In a room like this
   Mr Calantini
   Without smashing your fair share of *balls* first

   Pause.

   They say, Mr Calantini, that the arc of the moral universe
   bends towards justice
   That is the sentiment, at least, amongst my more… *idealistic*
   colleagues

   Beat.

   Marianne certainly thinks that
   And

I imagine
Roy probably felt that way once too
But that isn't me, Mr Calantini
That isn't who you're dealing with here

Beat.

They say that the arc of the moral universe bends towards
justice and yeah
Fine
That might well be true
I wouldn't know
I cannot speak to that
But what I do know, Mr Calantini
What I can speak to
One thing I do know
For sure
Is this

Beat.

The arc of the moral universe *may or may not* bend towards
justice, Mr Calantini
But I intend to make certain that it bends towards me
Towards me
Towards
Stephen

Beat.

And so you will bend too, Mr Calantini
Mark my words, by God and by my hand
This shit show that you've concocted here today will bend
towards my will
And so
God willing
Will you
And so
God willing
Will
You

He exits after MARIANNE. *A silence falls.*

ROY. Well I don't know what they're so stressed out about

Beat.

After all there are, like, seventy more cans now

CALANTINI. People don't work that way though do they?
People don't work logically
People don't work with that kind of interior linear logic
'This equals this'
They don't do that
Do they?

Beat, ROY *thinks.*

ROY. No
No, I guess they don't

Beat.

CALANTINI. I think they think... probably
Somewhere still, in their messed-up heads
I think
They deep down think they're probably still going to find
something worth finding
And
That it could very well be in this very can

Beat.

I mean
After all
Let's face it
It might as well be in this can

His face is now very close to the can.

If you follow their logic, that is
Because as far as they're concerned
As far as they can *think*
With their screwed-up, frightened little minds
What they're looking for
It could be anywhere
And despite the fact that it's almost certainly nowhere
It has just got to be somewhere
Right?

ROY. Umm yeah… Right

CALANTINI. And that 'somewhere'
That *'somewhere'*
Could be in this can, couldn't it?
In this can
That I've punctured
With this harpoon
And so the 'something that is somewhere' that they're still
hoping for…
That could be slowly rotting away now
In the air
In that can
And
Even though they know it's false about the 'secret
knowledge'
Even though they know that's false
They *feel* it's true
You know?

ROY. Right
Yeah sure
I guess

CALANTINI. And
Anyway
There aren't

Pause.

ROY. What?

CALANTINI. There aren't

ROY. There aren't what?

CALANTINI. Seventy cans of Bluefin tuna in my basement

Beat.

ROY. What?

CALANTINI. Yeah…

ROY. Wait…
    Wait…
    So that was…?

CALANTINI. That was bullshit

Pause.

ROY. Oh fuck!

CALANTINI. Yeah
    I know, right?

ROY. Oh…*fuck*

CALANTINI. That was just some crazy
    Crazy
    Thing I said

ROY. So your dad didn't…?

CALANTINI. Go round the world stockpiling Bluefin cans for
    personal consumption?
    No

Beat.

ROY. So does that mean that he didn't really…?

CALANTINI. Have a deeper understanding than anyone else
    about what might be in that can or, indeed, what special
    secret information might or might not be wrapped like a coil
    of bindweed around the Bluefin DNA helix?
    No
    He didn't

ROY. And so it's still possible…
    The 'secret knowledge'…
    That could…
    That could…

CALANTINI. That could be a thing
    Sure!
    Why not?

ROY. And it could be in that can right now?

CALANTINI. Sure
    Why not?
    That is assuming that it's Bluefin
    I'm not so sure

ROY. And that's the only can…?

CALANTINI. My guess is that it's Yellowfin
    Like a really fatty piece of Yellowfin?
    And that it showed up weird on the x-ray or something
    But hey
    Maybe I'm wrong
    Maybe my brother was buying Bluefin
    Or
    Maybe he just bought this one can and he hid it from me
    Or
    Maybe he thought it was Yellowfin
    I don't know
    I don't know anything about anything

ROY. But either way…

CALANTINI. But either way…

ROY. As far as you know

CALANTINI. As far as I know

ROY. That's the only can…

CALANTINI. Yeah

ROY. That's the only can with the potential…

CALANTINI. Yeah

    Beat.

ROY. Then why the fuck…?
    Why the fuck did you…?
    …let them think…?
    Why would you *do* that?!
    Why would you do that and then go and destroy that can?
    The only can?
    The only can that you have that might possibly be Bluefin?

The only can that you have
That *we* have
That might be able to tell us what we want to know?!
Why the fuck would you do that?!

CALANTINI. Because what difference would it make?
What difference would it make if it was Bluefin?
What difference would it make if it did have all the answers?
What good could possibly come from knowing that?
We're still us!
Knowing why the fish went won't change that!

Beat.

You heard him…
'We could be President, Marianne!'
It's all just the same shit

ROY. We have to try…

CALANTINI. No
No we don't
Why should we?
Try what?
What should we try?

ROY. We should try to make things better!
We should try to make things… back how they were!

CALANTINI. It's too late
It's too late for any of that
It is all too little
And it's all too late

ROY. But why would you lie?

CALANTINI *shrugs*.

CALANTINI. Because I had to do *something,* I guess

Beat.

ROY. Jesus
Jesus

Pause.

CALANTINI. It's Roy isn't it?

ROY. Yeah

CALANTINI. I'm Michael

Beat.

ROY. I'm pleased to meet you, Michael

CALANTINI. Yeah
I bet…

Pause.

Roy?

ROY. Yes, Michael?

CALANTINI. I miss my brother, Roy

Beat.

ROY. Yeah
Yeah I bet yah do, sport

Pause.

CALANTINI. Eat the tuna fish, Roy

Beat.

ROY. What?

CALANTINI. Eat the tuna
Eat it

Beat.

Here, look
I got this from my car

He takes a can opener out of his pocket and throws is across the room.

I keep my brother's old 'tool box' in the trunk
For old time's sake, y'know?
I got it out when I got the harpoon gun

Beat.

Use it
Open the can
Eat the tuna

Beat.

ROY. I...
Can't

CALANTINI. Oh
Sure you can

ROY. No

CALANTINI. Sure you can, Roy

ROY. ...I
...Really want to

CALANTINI. Of course you do
Why wouldn't you?

Beat.

The only thing you can do in this life is take a fucking can
opener to it
And open that fucking can
And eat as much of what you can from inside of that can
before anyone else gets a chance
Nothing else matters

Beat.

...Roy?

ROY. Yes, Michael?

CALANTINI. What difference could it make?
Really?
You've seen it all before
You've seen them, all before
You've seen the way that they behave
And so you know there's only one way this is going to go
And so you know that it really doesn't matter

Beat.

ROY. But it does matter
Doesn't it?

CALANTINI *shakes his head.*

CALANTINI. You're a human being, Roy
Act like one
Do what you gotta do
It's inevitable
Someone is going to eat this can of tuna
And it might as well be you

ROY. That doesn't make any sense

CALANTINI. Sure it does
In its own way
Sure it does
Here
I'll open it for you

He walks over to ROY, *who is sitting on the floor, his back against the desk, as though pinned. He picks up the can opener and takes it back to the table. He opens it, and throws the can on the floor by* ROY. *Beat.*

Roy?

ROY. Yeah?

CALANTINI. Fuck it
Roy

ROY *stares at the open can. Pause.*

ROY. Yeah?

CALANTINI. *Yeah*
Fuck it…
What does it matter, right?

Beat.

ROY. Right

Beat.

Oh shit
Oh shit, you're so right

Beat.

I wanna eat it

CALANTINI. So eat it
Fuck it

ROY. Yeah?
Yeah
Yeah!
Fuck it!
…Right?!

CALANTINI. Right!
Fuck it!

ROY. *Fuck it*

ROY *stares at the can for a long time.* CALANTINI *goes to* MARIANNE'*s place at the desk.*

CALANTINI. Roy…
What difference could it possibly make?

CALANTINI *presses the panic button under the desk, makes his way to the fire door and exits.* ROY *sits there for a moment. Time is now against him, he panics and launches at the tuna fish, eating it with his hands on all-fours.*

ROY. Oh shit
Oh shit the flakeage…

He eats and eats.

Oh yeah!

MARIANNE *re-enters through the double doors. She is visibly disgusted.*

MARIANNE. Roy?
Jesus Christ!
Jesus Christ, Roy!

ROY *looks at her and shrugs.*

ROY. Fuck it, Marianne
  Fuck it

MARIANNE. Jesus Christ
  Stephen!
  Stephen!

  MARIANNE *exits to find* STEPHEN, *whilst* ROY *continues to eat. The alarm sound fades out and 'Somewhere' from* West Side Story, *as sung by Matt Monroe, plays.* ROY *laughs and eats. Lights slowly fade to black.*

  The End.

A Nick Hern Book

Yellowfin first published in Great Britain as a paperback original in 2021 by Nick Hern Books Limited, The Glasshouse, 49a Goldhawk Road, London W12 8QP, in association with Jessie Anand Productions and Walrus Theatre

Yellowfin copyright © 2021 Marek Horn

Marek Horn has asserted his right to be identified as the author of this work

Cover artwork by Katie Allen

Designed and typeset by Nick Hern Books, London
Printed in Great Britain by Mimeo Ltd, Huntingdon, Cambridgeshire PE29 6XX

A CIP catalogue record for this book is available from the British Library

ISBN 978 1 83904 043 6

Woodland
CARBON
www.woodlandcarbon.co.uk
NICK HERN BOOKS
Printed on Carbon Captured paper